ROBERTO BENIGNI

Stefano Masi

Translated from the Italian by
Sandra Eiko Tokunaga

GREMESE

KU-602-160

PHOTO CREDITS
*All photos published in this book
are courtesy of the Agenzia Fotografica Dufoto of Rome,
except for those on p.p. 10, 11, 30, 33, 41, 44, 46, 47, 48, 49,
57, 58, 61, 62, 63, 64, 67, 68, 71, 73 and 74 (Centro Studi Cinematografici – Rome)*

Photocomposition and Photolithography:
Graphic Art 6 S.r.l. – Rome
E-mail: dva@uni.net

Printed and bound by: Grafiche Chicca & Co., S.n.c. – Tivoli

GREMESE
First Edition © 1999
New Books S.r.l.
Via Virginia Agnelli, 88 – 00151 Rome
Fax +39/(06)65740509
E-mail: gremese@gremese.com
Website: http://www.gremese.com

*All rights reserved. No part of this publication may be reproduced,
stored in a retrieval system, or transmitted in any form
or by any means, without the prior written permission
of the publisher.*

ISBN 88-7301-385-6

OMNI LIBRARY
FENDI

DU. foto   AGENZIA FOTOGRAFICA ITALIANA
00187 Roma - Piazza S. Silvestro, 13

Tel. +39 (06)6798964 – Fax +39 (06)6782668

CONTENTS

HIS 'UNCLE IN AMERICA' WAS NAMED OSCAR

To be ever smiling and simple, is the supreme art of life.
VLADIMIR MAYAKOVSKY

Three Oscars and seven nominations for *Life Is Beautiful* (*La vita è bella*, 1997): not even Fellini at his peak could boast such a score. No other foreign film had ever received seven nominations (*U-Boot 96* got six, along with Bergman's *Fanny and Alexander*). In any case, the Academy of Motion Picture Arts and Sciences did well in placing its stakes on Roberto Benigni, for he brought a breath of refreshing insanity to those rather stale annual proceedings held at the Dorothy Chandler Pavilion among cinema's hottest tabloid starlets and oldest embalmed dinosaurs. In fact, Associated Press even hinted that it might be the little Italian "devil" himself to present the next Academy Awards.

In the history of the Oscar, 1999 will definitely go down as the "Robordo" (as the Americans say it) Benigni year. With everyone dying to be seen with him. All eyes upon him. TV cameras tracking his every move, afraid of missing even just one of those star-struck, gasping mimics. Presenter Whoopi Goldberg, who might also be considered rather "benignesque" herself, quoted him constantly, keeping up a running dialogue of winks and nods from the stage. It was probably thanks to Roberto that the last Oscar ceremony of this millennium managed to break all records for duration time (four hours and two minutes) without boring the public to tears.

The organizers had nevertheless warned against over doing it *too* much. And as for Roberto, he had thought a lot about it: what could he do? Take his clothes off on stage? No. Slip the little statue into his pants pocket to simulate a super erection like he had done with the Coke bottle in *Berlinguer ti voglio bene* [Berlinguer, I love you, 1977]? Out of the question. Physically attack Sophia Loren, as he had done with Raffaella Carrà in Italy? Or else, lift her up and carry her off bodily in his arms? All of these had either already been done or else could never be. So he hit on another idea and promptly sat down in the last seat at the very end of the row, with that roguish look flashing in his eyes and his Princess Nicoletta right by his side. As Sophia tore open the envelope, she barely had time to cry out, "…and the Oscar goes to… Roberto!" that he sprung up with the masterfulness of an acrobat (as a matter of fact, as a boy he had spent a few months training in a provincial circus) and, balanced on the arms of his seat high above the sea of uplifted faces and their one great *Ohhhhhhh!* he took his first steps on the road to triumph right there in the Dorothy Chandler Pavilion. Just like that, leaping from the arm of one seat on to another, onto the backs of other seats, miraculously not trampling on anyone in front of him who, at the same time, were getting out of the way fast, fearing for their recent face lifts at the lightning advance of this crazy Italian. And, leap after leap, he even vaulted over Steven Spielberg, seated two rows in front of him, the "tough Spielberg" who had recently turned up his nose at *Life Is Beautiful* – such an anti-technological film.

Then finally, in one bound, landing on his two feet on the stairs of the stage, in a kangaroo hop, exactly as in one of the sequences of his film when he hops onto a desk to harangue a group of diligent school children in their Balilla uniforms.

"I want you! I want you!" Sophia cried, for a moment going along with Cioni Mario, a Benigni character, for whom "an old hen makes good broth" too. That is, before Roberto's appeal to higher sentiments: "I thank my parents in Vergaio, a small village in Italy, for the best gift, poverty!" Quite frankly, I found more honesty in the words he came up with when Helen Hunt presented him with statuette number two, the one for Best Actor, an award which truly caught him by surprise: "This is a terrible mistake… I used all my English… how can I express all my gratitude… My body is in tumult because everything is unexpressed."

In actual fact, Benigni now speaks quite acceptable English, even if he does still keep those foreigner's aphasia, which take the form of linguistic-poetic licenses which abound in the syntax of his Tuscan-English or Anglo-Tuscan utterances that give rise to the most delightful puns. For him language was never really a barrier, not even when he only knew three words of English and Jim Jarmusch had him act in *Down by Law,* or should we say, *Daunbailò* (1986): Roberto Benigni was the first artist to receive an Oscar for Best Actor for a performance in a film that was not in the English language.

> *Amidst the great mayhem of the Oscars, one thing remained fixed in the mind, for it had stirred an ancient emotion. Roberto Benigni was Pinocchio, leaping over the heads of spectators as he jumped upon the stage. If it is true that thought, in its being, can be but image, then this was the image of a thought so very childish, but precisely because of this, so very profound.*
> FURIO SCARPELLI, SCREENWRITER

And in his triumphant march, he defeated some pretty hefty English-speaking actors, from Tom Hanks to Ian McKellan.

This was one of the many challenges that *Life Is Beautiful* so unexpectedly overcame, an outsider which has now cashed in millions in the United States and has even managed to break the traditional reticence of the very serious Academy when it comes to film comedy. That is, if *Life Is Beautiful* can really be considered a comedy… Also extremely rare was the awarding of an Oscar to an actor who had directed himself: before Roberto, the only other instance was the great Laurence Olivier in distant 1948 with his screen version of *Hamlet*.

And now that Roberto has won them, what will become of the statuettes? Will he keep them in his apartment in Rome atop Aventino, or will he entrust them to Papa Gigi? And where will his father put them? Will he hide them in the vegetable garden, among the zucchini and lettuce, out of sight of any possible thieves, just as he had done with the Golden Globe Award? Something other than a strongbox! Farmers, as everyone knows, are much too clever to be fooled by city mice…

We make people laugh but we treat social, tragic themes, themes which involve the defenseless classes, revealing hidden injustices. I see something important in the Nobel Prize being awarded to me, and the Oscar to Benigni: poets, artists are no longer those who soar in the heights, but those who are also rooted in concrete and tragic reality. This is the recognition that the characterization of the comic is satirical and tragic.
DARIO FO, NOBEL PRIZE FOR LITERATURE

Roberto, indomitable.

A Question of Undershirts

The question now is, after three Oscars, will he still wear those ribbed undershirts? Personally, I hope so. There are some habits that California might change. Others not. For example, he will still suffer from insomnia (which is why you will almost never see him up and around in the morning) staying up very late,

Roberto in Life Is Beautiful.

until four or later in the morning, just like in the good ole days when his nights began in a round of Roman film clubs where he could peer deep into the woeful eyes of Buster Keaton. If you want to win him over, just say you want to bet on something. He is always ready for a wager: in his hometown of Vergaio it was the favorite sport.

A good way to kill time when summer was spent sitting around the little tables of the "Casa del Popolo," the Communist Party's gathering center, with Casaglieri (also known as Frank, the fascist police officer in a sequence in *Life Is Beautiful*), Taccone, Biagioni, Paccianti, and l'Antichi, and when anything was good for a bet: who could make it all around town on his Vespa driving down the streets the wrong way with his back up against the handlebars? Or who wanted to play blind man's bluff with death, that is, walking blindfolded for kilometers and at nightfall crossing the highway (as we see in the opening sequence of *Tuttobenigni* [All Benigni, 1986]: with the stakes up for the taking, about 200 dollars). Or else, who could get to Prato with a bottle of mineral water balanced on his head; or who could drive up to Viareggio and back, the whole time in fourth, without ever shifting gears, not even at traffic lights. As loose as Totò, as vulnerable and articulate as Woody Allen, as good on a tightrope as Groucho Marx, as bad as Pinocchio, this robust, disjointed, small-town kid was to become the layman saint of an entire generation of Italy's thirty to forty-year-olds. Those who some years before had "protested" against the Establishment and who today, at the turn of the millennium, have rather freehandedly taken up the reins of power and leadership of what is generally referred to as Italy's Second Republic.

Americans who have only just discovered him thanks to the seven nominations and three Oscars for *Life Is Beautiful* see Benigni as another emigrant of comedy from the Old World, like the London strolling player Charles Chaplin, whom the Tuscan filmmaker is starting to resemble more and more. For Benigni it was all the more difficult, especially with the hurdle of a different language (one that up to quite recently he did not speak at all), though he has miraculously turned even this to his advantage, managing to touch the hearts of people of all races and cultures and even succeeding in getting Americans to understand Dante's verses of the *Divine Comedy*.

Benigni shares with Chaplin not only a sense of pathos, but also an inner concealed maliciousness which seemingly inoffensive characters possess, who at first sight win you over by their vulnerability. Benigni "the tramp" of some of his films is Chaplin-like, just as is Benigni "the monster," who is innocent though never defenseless: "There is always a little maliciousness in my characters – I want to make them real, and so that also makes them mean." What he also has in common with Chaplin is his ability to be universal, by the use of an updated version of silent movie communication, made up of strong, expressive mimics, almost like a cartoon. And Benigni not only uses this mimicry in his films, but also in television

With Nicoletta Braschi in Life Is Beautiful.

> *I think it is more difficult to be a Russian Mastroianni than an Italian Woody Allen... what I would really like to be, though, is a Swiss Anna Magnani, but I can't seem to come up with the style to live up to her. What I am really aiming for is nevertheless the Swiss Anna Magnani...*

Woody Allen is still absolutely great, though he has become a little too goody-goody, he makes me think of a Gucci handbag. Too perfect. Before, he used to be dirtier. To dirty yourself a little, to give yourself without defenses is an act of generosity for a comic actor.

appearances, where he often acts like Roger Rabbit in his duos with Bob Hoskins, literally jumping into onlookers' arms.

In his own way (very much *his* own way, since Roberto Benigni is without question a rebel), he did demonstrate his excellent know-how when it came to using all the right vehicles of the world of American entertainment, television to start with. Indeed he became famous almost overnight, between the summer of 1998 and the spring of 1999.

In Italy, anyone who had been about twenty in '68 and had rooted for the Left (ninety percent of the Italian young people at the time), was later very moved to see a film courageous enough to be called *Berlinguer ti voglio bene* when it was released. It was 1977. Passions, ideologies and feelings were all one. Whoever voted Communist could never be caught with a right-wing girlfriend. Could not even have friends on the Right, since they were all "fascists." Roberto Bengini's first one-man show at the Teatro Alberichino in Rome would also remain linked to the Communist leader Enrico Berlinguer's name. Squeezed under a staircase, a small dark and damp space, a single light bulb flickering in the middle of the stage, here was this Tuscan farmer making his debut with Hamlet-like doubts on what syllable to stress in the Secretary of the Italian

Left and opposite: *Benigni as a young man at the Poets' Festival near the University of Rome.*

Dadddd. Oh, what are you doing all the time holed up in that toilet…? Oh how you close the door so carefully, oh… and even when Mom was alive – "Oh Giulia, I'm going for a crap"… "Oh Giulia, I'm going for a piss"… "Oh Giulia I'm going to comb my hair" – and then, one day she died. And that was really it… you never came out of there again… and then, it was ten minutes to eat and BAM! You were gone again: occupied! Before that, when Mom was around… before, every so often… I'd hear the two of you… oh sometimes you'd really be going at it! But now, it's hard-on, limp, hard-on… and then never again – for him! But for me… well, what would a man be without this little thing, huh? A big blob!? Big, small, big, small… they say "Ahh too many wanks!" One wank, too many wanks… I get on the bus and just the swaying gives me a hard-on. All the bus routes: I've got that subscription ticket for three thousand lire… but I still say the most beautiful thing that exists in Italy today is a cunt.

FROM *CIONI MARIO DI GASPARE FU GIULIA*

Communist Party's last name: "BERLinguere, BerLINguere, BerlinGUERRE…" and then, a flood of obscenities, despairing, desperate, images of the ordinary madness of an impassioned Tuscan communist from the rural sub-proletariat.

A few years later, when he finally did meet Berlinguer in

person at a Party rally, Benigni hugged him and carried him off in his arms: *the* Enrico Berlinguer… That crazy snap appeared in all the magazines, but not because Benigni was a famous actor, no, no, he was a complete unknown. The star was Enrico Berlinguer, Secretary of the Italian Communist Party, one of the few Italian politicians truly cherished in the hearts of the Italian people.

Images of a distant past. Today Berlinguer is no more, nor is the Italian Communist Party, though from them the "Quercia" (Oak) and the "Ulivo" (Olive) have sprung, in a political movement that is moral heir to the Italian workers' movement though in an increasingly more watered-down way. The "marginal" Benigni, who at the time was a provocative regular on an offbeat TV show hosted by Renzo Arbore, is today a blockbuster who has raked in billions of lire at the Christmas box office, in a progressive Italy led by an equally modern left-wing government. With *kommunism* no more, that ogre which ate children alive, the most Communist comic in all of Italy is today plastered across the Wall Street Journal's front pages – making his rounds as he shakes hands with America's motion-picture tycoons in California, the powerful Jewish "clique" in Hollywood, magnates prepared to invest fabulous sums in the planet's film business, and who were so moved by his *Life Is Beautiful*.

Despite his dialectal speech, over the previous fifteen years Benigni had managed to work in American films. He had frayed two separate paths across the Atlantic: one to old Hollywood and the other to the independent film world. "Pink Panther" Sellers had passed him the torch and Roberto was directed by the master of Hollywood comedy, Blake Edwards; he had teamed up with veteran Walter Matthau. But Roberto also won over a cult-film director with quite a young following, Jim Jarmusch. And then he was cast in the last film made by Fellini, *Voices of the Moon* (*La voce della luna*, 1990). Who would ever have dreamed of such a career for this down-and-out strolling player who in the seventies was haunting Rome's underground theatres with people such as Lucia Poli and Marco Messeri?

Even while collecting success after success, he has never betrayed his own personal vocation. And though he is now a true box-office champion in the Cecchi Gori stables (*Life Is*

> *Californians are convinced they've invented Neapolitan pizza. Which means they can also convince themselves that Roberto Benigni is the heir to Chaplin.*
>
> GIULIANO FERRARA, JOURNALIST

Beautiful has broken all previous box-office records for an Italian film, both in Italy and abroad), in his live appearances Roberto has continued to turn the Italian language and the nation inside out with his ferocious monologues. In 1996 there he was spitting his venom over the symbols of a bigot Italy, from Silvio Berlusconi to Giuliano Ferrara, his arch-enemy. Perhaps the Oscars and presumed "do-goodism" of *Life Is Beautiful* will mellow Benigni's more incisive ways.

Nevertheless the little devil of Vergaio has always had that miraculous capacity to transform the most obscene language into poetry, as in his *Hymn of a Loose Body*, poem-song dedicated to the joys of defecating (a free translation of which might go something like this: "Wiping your ass brings joy divine / with leaves of pumpkin, beet-greens or vine / So go and crap for it is demonstrated / you wipe your ass when you have defecated! / Hurray for latrines, blessed they be / Hurray for the restroom, toilet, WC / Hurray for fields awaiting manure / Long live shit, and its crappers for sure!").

It is true that extremes meet. For it was Benigni himself, precisely the one to have come just one step from excommunication when he addressed the very serious Pope on TV with a disrespectful epithet (something to the effect of "that ole Wotyla… !" making RAI's chiefs and directors at the time tremble behind their desks), and the one who had played a leading role in Arbore's blasphemous film *Il Pap'occhio* [a play on words for "the Pope" and "a big mess", 1980] who was actually summoned to the Vatican when His Holiness desired a private viewing of *Life Is Beautiful*. And the supreme pontiff's emotion swept away any grudges: "ole Wotyla's" tears beatified

Above and opposite: *A live performance, a dimension where Roberto is in his element.*

Benigni and even the Catholic press was rooting for him during the final lap to the Oscars, *Famiglia Cristiana* [Christian Family] leading the way. As is commonly known, madness is a cousin to saintliness. Moreover, besides his streak of craziness, Roberto Benigni also brings to cinema the stigmata of an extremely poor childhood. This is something he shares in common with many great comedians of popular tradition, from Totò to Charlie Chaplin, whose natural heir he seems to be, particularly after his veering to pathos in this last film. As sediment in the "little

As corporal in the Tenth Lancers, I was captured by the Nazis after the armistice with the Allies. In the work camp I suffered from cold, hunger and fear. I had spoken about it a thousand times to Roberto. But what they were doing to the Jews, at the time, I knew nothing about that. Only recently with Roberto have I understood what was going on at a hair's breadth.
GIGI BENIGNI, ROBERTO'S FATHER

devil's" imagination are also reminiscences of an almost mythic peasant poverty, woven through with mystery, pagan fantasy, a magical physicality, not even remotely idyllic, where animals, men and the fruit of the earth all fecundated together in the same primordial mire. "We all slept in the same bed, ours was one of those families of heroic starvation. Our entire fortune consisted of three or four ducklings," recalls Roberto. His parents, Gigi and Isolina, both Tuscans, his father was from Frassineto, his mother from Pergognano, had married in 1942, at the height of the War. Gigi donned his military uniform right after their wedding and departed for the Albanian front. He managed to survive that close confrontation with death and even the Nazi work camps in Germany. Three daughters were first born to the Benigni household: Albertina, Bruna and Anna Lucia. After that, little "Robertino," on 27 October 1952, under the sign of the Scorpion, ascendant Capricorn. He was given the middle name Remigio, after his paternal grandfather. Roberto Benigni dedicated an affectionate homage to his family in an autobiographical sequence in *Down by Law*, in which he recalled the death of a wild rabbit at the loving hands of Mamma Isolina armed "with rosemary, olive oil, garlic and other secrets."

For years the Benigni family worked the master's land on the farm owned by Count Serristori (a famous wine producer), in a town with the colorful name of Misericordia, in the commune of Castiglione Fiorentino. Gigi, Isolina their four children, together with other relatives' families, all farmhands, lived in a huge farmhouse where the Benigni's occupied a couple of rooms. "Both my Mom and my Dad had stepmothers and stepfathers who also had many other children. We were forty or fifty in the same house, just like in the 1800s."

Though by the time Robertino was born, Papa Gigi was no longer a shareman, and only owned a small patch of land, tilling the fields of other farmers for what was about half a dollar a day. Occasionally he went to work as a hand on the railroad.

Robertino's early childhood was spent playing outside, slipping away barefoot to the fields, to the cowshed, through the hedges, amidst the geese and cackling hens. "I also remember a big chimney and a roaring fire, which I spent a lot of time playing with, since I have burns on every part of my body. I was attracted, as all children are, to two things: fire and excrement." Once Robertino even managed to fall into the cesspool, in a sea of excrement so thick that a small child could easily have been swallowed up and lost his life. Apparently that big bath of shit was to bring him good luck… Robertino was just five when the family "emigrated" from Valdichiana, where the rural economy was in crisis, to Galciana where the region's first industries were concentrated. The Benigni's had heard that there was plenty of work for everyone there, even for the women. Papa Gigi rented a truck and loaded it up with the family, furniture, mattresses, household effects, rabbits, chickens, all the meager family possessions. That very day, after three months of drought, the sky unleashed a pouring rainstorm, as if out of spite. Papa Gigi, Mamma Isolina, Robertino and his three elder sisters all climbed into the cabin of the truck for shelter.

Along the way they passed some traffic police who were left dumbfounded to see how a family of six could successfully squeeze into the cabin of one truck. That trip, though only a few dozen kilometers, nevertheless stayed fixed in little Roberto's memory: it was like an ocean crossing. Indeed in his imagination it meant a tremendous upheaval. In the Arezzo area, where the Benigni family set up house, the dialect had a very different resonance than the one spoken in Valdichiana. Robertino, landing up in elementary school there, was considered almost like an immigrant. "I listened to Pratese and it sounded to me the same way as American English does now. It was incomprehensible even though it was Tuscan too."

He was a bright child bursting with life. At the age of three he could already point out the regions of Italy on a map; at six he would dive under the teacher's desk to try to get a look up

her skirt; at ten he was already writing exceptional compositions. They were so good, in fact, that the principal called his parents in to compliment them. More often than not, however, they were summoned to the school because Robertino had pulled yet another one of his practical jokes, some being pretty bad.

It was absolutely freezing in their new house in Galciana, "Via fra i Campi." Papa Gigi signed a wad of promissory notes and bought a kerosene stove. The bedroom (one for all six) was adjoined to the stables. It was 1958. The Benigni family soon discovered that their hopes for well-being had been completely unfounded. That year turned out to be the worst since the war for the area's small industries. Isolina could find no work. Gigi was laid off from his job at a local company. In a desperate attempt to make ends meet, he went to the rag-pickers of Prato to rummage through sacks received from all over the world. He pulled out jackets and pants in good enough condition, bought them up by the kilo and sold them to the farmers of Valdichiana, not in exchange for cash, but for chickens. Then, he turned around and sold the chickens to wealthy Prato, where he could offer much more competitive prices than the local butchers.

In the meantime, Robertino, despite his liveliness, was much too thin and was simply not growing. He was so small, so very little that the family called him "Small Change," not only because of his size, but also since he would go around town asking anyone he ran into for coins for candy.

"Small Change" had very bad sight and even his teeth were falling out. Not being able to afford the expense of fortifying treatments that the petty bourgeois families of the city weaned their offspring on, Gigi and Isolina took their little one to a peasant healer, the sorcerer Berni di Manciano, an expert in treating organ disorders with medicinal herbs, and who had also treated Robertino's elder sisters. The pagan side of peasant religiosity was strongly imprinted in his mind and would re-emerge later in his monologues on religion, regarded apparently as offensive by orthodox Catholics, but which in fact reveal a very deep knowledge of the Old Testament. The second reading of the biblical episodes of the Creation by Benigni in his 1995-1996 tour, traces of which have been preserved both in his second film, *Tuttobenigni 95-96* (a film-concert produced by Melampo, under the technical direction of film editor Claudio Cutry) and in the small anthology published by Einaudi *E l'alluce fu* [And there was light], are one of the musts of the little Tuscan devil.

The Bible – one of the few books which were kept by the firesides of all farmhouses – resurfaces every so often in Benigni's imagination, such as during his readings of Dante, whether in Italy or in America, when he might suddenly suggest a few curious analogies between highlights from the Good Book and the *Divine Comedy*.

The Crazed Look of Horses

Legends, fables, nursery rhymes, lunar cycles, rural witches. The magic of peasant life was like an open book. An absolutely

I liked it when people laughed, and I really felt that this was the only reason for my being there. My only concern was amazement, wonder, of how to astound people so that they would laugh: whatever people laughed at seemed to me the only thing worth doing, it was what gave me the most satisfaction.

fascinating book. On winter evenings the Benigni family gathered around the fireplace, one of those huge ones like a little house: in Robertino's eyes it seemed like a cave in hell! Grandfather played the accordion. The elders sang *ottavine*, a tradition of popular Tuscan poetry. They all improvised verses and short popular chants called *stornelli*, or nonsensical *corbellerie* in rhyme. And these marked the beginnings of Roberto's artistic training as a future strolling player, around those firesides. And then, there were also the rural celebrations with winding processions that made their way along the streets, meant to give thanks for the crop, for the reaping, the grape harvest, any pretext to make merry in the village square.

Roberto, as mentioned, was an extremely bright little boy at school and showed exceptional imagination in his compositions, some of which quite ingenious. Papa Gigi always likes to tell of Roberto's Italian teacher who was left flabbergasted by a composition he had submitted on Yuri Gagarin. "He said not even a teacher would have been able to write something like that…" But more than anything, Roberto loved making his classmates laugh. He would even sell them his jokes at the very reasonable price of ten lire apiece.

And yet life was really no laughing matter. The Benignis' financial situation was that of utter poverty, even if things did slightly improve after they left Galciana and moved to Vergaio (where *Berlinguer ti voglio bene* was shot, as well as the exteriors for *Tuttobenigni*), not far from Prato. This was in the heart of the

Above and opposite: *Dishevelled and intentionally slipshod in his live shows.*

The circus was a brief experience I had when I was 13 or 14 years old, at the end of junior high. A circus came to town, to Vergaio, it was called Circo Modin. And so, since we were on vacation, well I didn't exactly run away, but let's say I just took off for a few weeks with the circus.

textile area which was in rapid expansion and starting to offer some employment opportunities.

As Robertino became of age, he picked up all the ways of the town's youths, such as billiard games at the local bar. And then, there were the hours and hours they spent playing cards. They say that Roberto, being so clever and also so needy, managed to fleece quite a few people in those days. But when he lost?

Desperately broke as usual, he would sometimes slink off to the WC and climb out the window, just as he later did in a vaguely autobiographical sequence in *Il minestrone* [Minestrone, 1981] by Franco Citti.

After junior high, he was sent to study in Florence, Via Giovanni Pascoli, in a Jesuit school. On Sundays in church he played the organ and even read the Scriptures. But the Jesuits' discipline was far too inflexible for a youngster like Roberto. Someone remembers how he used to chase after the nuns for fun, teasing them with "Donna baffuta sempre piaciuta," a popular saying about the eternal appeal of women with moustaches. A little devil's gag. He was rescued from the Jesuits by the flood of 1966 which devastated Florence and forced his return home. He studied accounting in Prato, at the Istituto per il Commercio Francesco Datini ("the one who invented the promissory note," he explains). But there, Roberto did not limit himself to studying invoicing and balance sheets. He also started organizing his first cabaret evenings at a place nearby lent to him by the Ridotto del Metastasio. Five or six guitar chords were enough to create a perfect accompaniment for his nonsensical rhymes. For Roberto, this was a return to the peasant tradition of the *ottavine*, improvisations in octaves composed by the "Bernescantis" (a name chosen in memory of the sixteenth-century poet Francesco Berni, whose heirs they considered themselves). The show did not go unnoticed.

Actually those cabaret evenings at the Ridotto del Metastasio were not really his very first appearances as an artist, since he had also once spent a few weeks traveling with a small circus, sometimes performing as an apprentice clown and even as an acrobat. More often than not, however, he appeared as the magician's helper. "What's your name?" the magician would ask him. And Benigni, "I was called Roberto before, but now I'm Maria." And then there was the desert scene, another standard of provincial magicians. "We're in the Sahara, see how hot it is?" And he would start taking his clothes off. When his strip-tease got down to his shorts, the magician would suddenly change climates. "We're at the North Pole." And Roberto, sneezing, hastily put his clothes back on again.

At the Istituto Commeciale, Roberto liked the literature courses most of all, he managed to pass in economics and law, floundered in math, and was terrible in English. When not hitting the books or spending time with the circus, he worked as a barman at the Casa del Popolo of Vergaio, a place where hoodlums of every kind hung out, some of them ready to act on any crazy *corbellerie* just to shake up that small gray town turning upon itself in circles.

Being behind a bar has many things in common with being on stage, and every barman is in a way called upon to "entertain" his customers, many of whom are often, themselves, another show within the show. Roberto was mentally photographing faces, obsessions, tics: a sampling of characters and stories that later proved extremely useful in recounting the life, works and miracles of Cioni Mario, the provincial anti-hero of *Berlinguer ti voglio bene*. But as far as Roberto Benigni was concerned, provincial life also meant the death of any artistic aspiration. To leave was a moral obligation… He had already been to Milan once, trying to break into the circle of the "Celentano Clan." Singer-composer? Yes, why not? After all, he did play the harmonica, organ, guitar, and could also compose songs. He had even gotten a little band together with some friends once, though without any money it soon broke up. But Roberto had not wanted to give up his singing ambitions and had found an impresario who had made

him a few vague promises. He even managed to get ripped off by a million lire (about five-hundred dollars, all of Papa Gigi's hard-earned savings) by a record company in Alessandria who promised to make a record for him. The recording never saw the light.

After graduating in 1972, Roberto enrolled in university as a biology student. On 4 January of the same year, however, he also made his debut as an actor on the stage of the Teatro Metastasio in the play *Il re nudo* [The naked king] by the Teatro Studio, a troupe of talented young amateur players, including Nello Rossati, Pamela Villoresi and Saverio Marconi. Roberto only had a bit part, but the experience made him more than ever convinced that he was destined for the stage. Acting gave him tremendous pleasure, one of those "sexual joys that fill your whole body." At the Teatro Studio he met his contemporary Carlo Monni, who also came from a peasant background ("a family who had the best pigs in the region, absolutely"), and they would team up to perform at the rural patron-saint feasts.

The special routine of the Monni-Benigni team, though, was the bogus political rally at the Communist party's Festa dell'Unità meetings. They would go up on stage a half an hour before the real rallies and would start improvising a false one, as a joke, weaving in duos and monologues of hilarious ferocity. A few of these have been kept on video in *Tuttobenigni 95-96*, when Roberto appeals to the audience with his, "Electors and Electricians…"

There was also Donato Sannini, a bearded young man from Florence, to share in their artistic ambitions. He was the grandson of Countess Flavia Farina Cini who had once run a famous acting school (Donato Sannini died at hardly thirty-eight and Roberto Benigni remembered him in a dedication in the credits of his most ingenious film *The Little Devil* (*Il piccolo diavolo*, 1988).

On 4 September 1972, together with Monni, Sannini, and the set designer Aldo Buti, Roberto Benigni left Tuscany to try his luck in Rome. For him it was like a voyage similar to young Chaplin's setting out for the Americas.

BREAD, LOVE AND DRAMA

Rome in the early seventies was a flourishing hub of intense avant-garde theatre activity. Donato Sannini, who had good connections in artistic circles and mountains of costumes inherited from his grandmother, managed to get the group booked at the underground theatres most in vogue in the capital, such as Teatro dei Satiri and Beat '72. They could not really consider themselves a true theatre company, but only a group of *guastatori*, or "hellraisers." And, as such, they chose to be referred to as "Il fantasma dell'Opera" ["The Phantom of the Opera"]. The first show they performed, *I burosauri* [The burosaurs] by Silvano Ambrogi, was staged at the Teatro dei Satiri on 15 October 1972 with repeat performances at the Rondò di Bacco in Florence, as well as other theatres. Sannini directed, Buti did the set designs. Roberto and Monni, besides acting, thought up the texts. They ate little, slept little, earned little (nothing), and talked an awfully lot.

In *I burosauri* Roberto had a supporting role, but still managed to steal a bit of the show. Not too many remember it was him, however, in the gaudy dragoon officer's uniform (with golden shoulder straps he kept shaking every second with the greatest self-satisfaction), which he put on right after intermission. During the period from 1972 to 1976 Roberto haunted the circles of the Italian avant-garde theatre though not without some perplexity. ("To me they all seemed to be, and I'm not being ironic, no really, at the time like a comedy show. But I didn't think the funniness was involuntary, I thought it was intentional. Apparently that wasn't the case, though, from what

they told me.") He rubbed shoulders with some of the greats such as Leo De Berardinis, Perla Peragallo, Carmelo Bene, Giuliano Vasilicò and Memé Perlini. He acted in plays written by Lucia Poli, and appeared with her in *Le fiabe del Basile* [Fables of Basile] and *Le metamorfosi* [Metamorphoses] at the Teatro San Genesio, *La contessa e il cavolfiore* [The countess and the cauliflower] at the Teatro dei Satiri, *La festa* [The party] at the Beat '72; and Marco Messeri's plays, *Bertoldo Azzurro* at the Rondò di Bacco and *Mi voglio rovinare* [I want my own ruin] for the Decentramento Casertano. "All for free," Roberto recalls today with a sigh, when at the time he was such a desperately penniless young man.

In 1974, with the decline of "Il fantasma dell'Opera," he

I still read Rabelais, which is one of the most beautiful things, full of poetry, I often reread Ariosto, because he's funny and because I like the rhymes. I like rhyming poetry most of all, hidden rhymes less. It seems to me that to write poetry without rhyme is like playing tennis without a net or making love with your clothes on.

In fact, working with Roberto was like playing with a very young child who was just learning to talk. I was fascinated just listening to him. He made me laugh, he made me cry, but most of all laugh. And after a while I realized that inside this child there was a film.
GIUSEPPE BERTOLUCCI, DIRECTOR

joined Lucia Poli, her friend Giuseppe Bertolucci, and the set designer Buti to form a new troupe, with the sporadic participation of Donato Sannini, *Le parole e le cose* [Words and objects] intended to go beyond image-theatre to set new expressive forms. His encounter with Giuseppe Bertolucci proved to be decisive. For it was Bertolucci who got Roberto to tame the raging torrent of his emotions, to link it all to the history of theatre and literature. He encouraged Roberto to read and digest authors such as Collodi, Schopenauer, Whitman, Dostoyevsky, Rabelais. Indeed Roberto, at the time with his background from the Istituto Commerciale, had a burning desire to know the classics of literature and approached them with a fresh new look.

In Walt Whitman's verses, Roberto rediscovered a physical vision of love bound to the forces of nature; in *Notes from the Underground*, he found an example of a narrative stream in which the ego revealed itself, mysterious and domineering; in *Gargantua*, the comic yet poetic expression of an animalistic physicality. The combined influence of these three writers resulted in that mixture of panic-stricken religiosity, exasperated sensuality, and poetic lightness which all go into the making of the "Benigni touch."

Left: A bit of relaxation!

It was with Bertolucci, in October of 1974, that Roberto wrote the script for *Cioni Mario di Gaspare fu Giulia* [Cioni Mario of Gaspare, the late Giulia], a show in which he reconciled his avant-garde experiences with his continued passion for the less tamer art of cabaret. "Roberto and I spent five days alone, in Casarola, my village in the Apennines," recalls Giuseppe Bertolucci, "it was raining. The pink room had a French door through which you looked out onto only the green of a great ascending meadow. We stayed locked up in that room for five days. He talked non-stop spitting out stories, characters, images, ideologies, poetry. I listened and searched for a thread in all that flow of accented end-syllables and truncated lines. I was searching for a thread and I found a whole world: the universe of the poor outskirts of provincial Tuscany, communist, peasant, sub-proletarian, and genital." Through the character of Cioni, all the anxieties and popular anger, all the existential frustrations of a child of the common people are brought to life. A child who has all the expressive force of the peasant culture running through his veins, and who, with his eyes filled with fierce amazement, gazes upon middle-class Italy with its clumsy myths and commonplaces. Riotous obscenities, fantastic oaths, writhing guts, a rainbow of blasphemies, mountains of four-letter words, gigantic sexual abuses, are turned into poetry in a death dealing monologue that slams into the public with the violence of a tractor. The first performance, staged at the Circolo Arci in a small town near Vergaio, created scandal amidst the speechless public, for the most part peasant farmers and laborers. The following day the president of the Circolo was forced to resign. But Paolo Poli was also in the audience and, far from being shocked, he had even broke out into applause at the talent of this wild bold Tuscan. In December 1975 the show was received with praise at the Teatro Alberichino in Rome, giving Roberto his first taste of theatrical renown.

The jump from theatre to television was a small one. Among the enthusiastic fans of Roberto's unruly verve was Massimo Fichera, enlightened chief of RAI's young Channel 2, a station particularly interested in new faces and emerging

Above and opposite: *The "divo" gives in to photographers…*

artists. Fichera became Benigni's most important sponsor and the one who made those first important television appearances possible. In 1976 Roberto even dared to ask him for a daily thirty-second spot at the end of the news program, a truly "indecent proposal," which was of course rejected. Cioni Mario made it to television thanks to *Vita da Cioni* [A Cioni life], a program written by Benigni together with Giancarlo Governi. The Tuscan actor teamed up with his longtime buddy Carlo Monni for the show. Nevertheless, judged "too courageous," the program stayed shelved at the RAI until 1978. Another satirical broadcast, perhaps even more ferocious, appeared before that. It was written by Roberto Benigni, Beppe Recchia and Umberto Simonetta. The first vehement title of the show, *Televacca* [Telecow], was eventually "toned down" to *Onda libera* [Free wave] but it still remained scandalous, so much so that one of the characters

(don Giordano played by Marco Messeri) was dropped to avoid complications.

Nevertheless, Benigni's television popularity only truly burst forth when Renzo Arbore made him the hero of the cult program L'altra domenica [A different Sunday], one of the first alternative TV shows aimed at rejuvenating the kitsch scene of Sunday entertainment, outside the realm of Pippo Baudo's "dictatorship," starched shirts and showgirl lineups.

In the role of an armchair film critic who sits back and lavishes muddled interpretations of films he has never seen, Benigni made his grand entrance onto the Italian cultural scene. Twisted logic (and body), aborted thoughts, all under the constant menace of a profane scurrility, only hinted at by Roberto but feared so greatly by the presenter Arbore, who conducted his "child prodigy" almost as if he were waving a baton. Indeed, at the time, film critics were a new myth for Italian culture, and they were so new that no one had ever

Roberto has been gifted with perspicacity and culture, precious qualities also when it comes to making people laugh. And then, he has an extraordinary memory, an incredible physicality that makes it fascinating just watching him, when he talks, gesticulates, or simply when he eats, runs, shows his profile.

Renzo Arbore, presenter

dared "fire on" on them before. Benigni with his desecrating violence – nevertheless tempered for the Sunday time-slot of the show – tore them apart with relish.

Some people (very few to be quite honest) had already seen him in the film *Berlinguer ti voglio bene*, released on the sly in very few cinemas, and which was a revised screen version of *Cioni Mario*. However everyone, but truly everyone, saw Roberto at the 1980 Sanremo Festival, where he was the crazy presenter of the last evening, together with Olimpia Carlisi, another Roman underground muse. This was when he made the RAI chiefs all break out in a cold sweat with his risky line on Pope John Paul II (the famous "ole Wotyla!..."), the Pope, of course, being considered absolutely off-limits for television comedy.

From time to time his ambition to be a singer, which he had never completely given up, reappeared: Roberto had not hung his guitar up for good and, from 1976 to 1986 he regularly performed at the singer-composer festival "Rassegna della canzone d'autore," organized by the Tenco Club. Other than the famous *Hymn of a Loose Body*, over the years he performed *Ernesta*, *La marcia degli incazzati* [Ernesta, The march of the pissed off] and *Mi piace la moglie di Paolo Conte* [I like Paolo Conte's wife] which were much applauded.

Between Wanks and Screws

At the Istituto Commerciale Datini, there were practically all girls in Roberto's class. To be surrounded by girls, just like at home where he had grown up with three older sisters, did not dampen his curiosity when it came to the opposite sex. In fact it exasperated it. In Benigni's imagination the mystery of womanhood, with that little pouch so jealously kept tucked away in the womb, was the fulcrum of the world. A view of sex which went back to the closed, mysterious vision of archaic peasant culture.

Remember Roberto's astonished expression when he peeks under the skirt of the heroine in a scene from *The Monster* (*Il mostro*, 1994)? If Totò had eternal, atavistic hunger sparkling in his eyes as he stuffed fistfuls of spaghetti in his jacket pockets, Benigni has the infinite lust for sex expressed in his actions, and above all in his words, the purest obscenities that fill his mouth and which miraculously never slip into vulgarity. On the contrary, there is always a veil of poetry in the tales of his fucking ("We're the kind of people who don't screw very much. We're the kind of people who pack the cinemas to see nude women and go home and wank," declares Carlo Monni in *Berlinguer ti voglio bene*), talking about asses, "pussies" but most of all wanks ("Too many wanks. Too many wanks, one wank," says Cioni Mario on the stage of the Alberichino).

What's the main difference between a man and a woman? This was a topic of discussion at the "Mayakovsky" Casa del Popolo of Vergaio in the film *Berlinguer ti voglio bene*. For Cioni the question didn't exist. "For me, women are men too, since a man with a cunt is a woman." Men, women, parents, animals, pumpkins. It's all grist to the mill in the teleology of this sub-proletarian Tuscan. For a wicked humanity, for the hoodlums wandering back and forth between the outdoor dance rink to the motorway overpasses (where, in later years, stones would be hurled onto passing cars), fantasizing about imaginary fucks, "getting laid," was the universe's ultimate purpose, the mythical goal of existence. Through Cioni Mario and his gang of sub-proletarian good-for-nothings, Benigni expressed the despair of his provincial contemporaries who, after the devastation of peasant culture by the mass media, were sinking into the swamps of the contemporary void, though nevertheless at the same time spreading the seeds of that archaic violence which until then had been left slumbering within the bounds of farmyard fences.

In a world so seemingly well educated, measured, and politically correct, where people committed murder with a smile on their lips, the immoderate sexual vitality of acrobat Roberto Benigni became an antidote people realized they could not live without. *Berlinguer ti voglio bene* is still the film that shows the most "free-range" and violent side of his obsessions, which appeared in increasingly gentler forms in subsequent screenplays and characters, as he came closer and closer to becoming that "layman saint" of progressive Italy.

In the sub-proletarian Tuscany of *Berlinguer ti voglio bene*, between squalid outdoor dance rinks and the Case del Popolo and their "cultural" discussions, even the relationship between man and earth passes through an infinite hunger for sex, the ultimate expressive demonstration, craved by all but forbidden to most. A desire which was an end in itself, denied, blocked, acquiring virulence precisely because of its impossible fulfillment. There was an air of incest in families and zoophilous insinuations in the stalls. Any hole was good enough. This was not the luminous fairy-tale Tuscany of

> *He liked girls far too early. The first was a certain Cristina. But that wasn't anything to boast about, we have always liked women. Always in the right way, not for those things that you see in films nowadays, that television really shouldn't show — but love, yes.*
> GIGI BENIGNI, PAPA DI ROBERTO

popular actor Leonardo Pieraccioni's films, but rather the dark and fearful one of serial killers, such as the monsters of the Pacciani case. Here even the sacred myth of the mother was soiled – like a Carmelo Bene provocation – by the image of a hooker, even if it was with a heavy heart, as when Cioni Mario in *Berlinguer ti voglio bene* gives his mother to Bozzone (Carlo Monni) to pay back a gambling debt. And it was Luigi Benigni himself – Roberto's father – who played the role in the film of the materialistic farmer who offered his crippled daughter's hand to a diabolical character just to get his hands on a patch of land. Possessions, land, blind sex, darkest incest. A peasant society that had never heard of idyllic Arcadia.

CIONI GOES TO CINECITTÀ

Produced by Antonio Avati and Gianni Minervini, *Berlinguer ti voglio bene* turned out to be pretty much a box-office fiasco. It was circulated normally in Tuscany, but other than that, the film was only screened with lukewarm response in Milan, Turin and Rome. The distributor Euro, made no effort to promote the film.

Whereas his television characters – sweetened up – were appealing trendsetters, the motion-picture Benigni still seemed too bitter, too lethal to be easily digested by the general public. Perhaps Roberto's comedy was too markedly "spoken" to bend to the visual language of films? That was what some people suggested. Yet, he protested, "To me, cinema is talk. To say that it is image is idiotic. Intervention in films happens through language. How did God intervene in the world? With the Word. He never said, "The world is image." And Michelangelo when he made Moses, he didn't say, "Why can't you see?" he said, "Why don't you speak?" To say that cinema is image is as banal as saying that radio is a media that is listened to. There are so many things to see in radio, just as there are so many things to listen to in cinema."

Though *Berlinguer ti voglio bene* was not successful, Roberto was immediately approached for another film project, an even bigger production, *La verità*, [The Truth]. This was to be the first film the aged but evergreen screenwriter Cesare Zavattini, at

He was supposed to make three films with me: the first for 4 million, the second for 8, and the third for 16. Unfortunately Berlinguer ti voglio bene *was released a year later than planned, because of financial trouble. At the time my business was small, and I had to find a partner to come up with 50% to produce the film. But the Countess Cicogna's company, Euro, was not able to meet its commitments, And so, when shooting was completed, the entire cost – 190 million [lire] – was left to me. The prohibiting of the film for children under 18, still in force today, was the final blow.*

GIANNI MINERVINI, PRODUCER

the time in his seventies, was going to direct. RAI 2 was to produce it, the channel where Benigni had made himself his little niche. The two met, talked, talked, talked, discussed a rough outline of the story: a guy goes to a TV network for a job,

Left: *Nicoletta Braschi and Roberto Benigni in a scene from* The Little Devil.

We liked each other a lot [...] I was there for five or six months, maybe even longer, without ever saying a word, since in the beginning he had had me do all the talking and then had said: now just watch me and when we do the screenplay, you can step in completely. So I shut up for six months and listened and watched Zavattini like a live film, eating with him, almost sleeping with him. I lived with his family, watched him work, paint, watched him compose poetry. And this seemed to me the most beautiful thing that could ever have happened to anyone. And then suddenly we fought, but not really a fight, I have some letters here from Zavattini that are veritable paintings, beautiful...

but is overcome with panic and flees. The story takes off from this escape, a kind of road picture, maybe in a truck, mysterious encounters, mishaps one after another.

In the spring of '78, the Zavattini-Benigni project was considered imminent, but afterwards everything became very iffy. Production was postponed several times and the film finally saw the light only four years later, without Benigni, and under the title *La veritàààà* (1982).

And thus the union with Zavattini was a *coitus interruptus*, for it did not produce any concrete fruits in Benigni's filmography. And yet, today, it can be said that moods of "Zavattinian" fantasy can be noticed here and there in Benigni's films, from *The Monster* right up to *Life Is Beautiful*. Nothing you can pinpoint, of course. But the way the "little devil" of Vergaio sees and reconstructs reality seems to have absorbed Zavattini's

Opposite: *A moment of reflection for the "little devil."*

magic. Those smiling bums who, armed with happiness and a kind of wisdom, mounted their brooms and took to the skies in *Miracle in Milan* (*Miracolo a Milano*, 1951) could just as well have been the uncles (perhaps twice removed) of some of Benigni's creatures and their illuminations. In both instances they "take flight" with the same lightness, passing severe judgment on the world, history, our society. This is a poetic invitation very far removed from the tastes of Italian comedy, and which might be termed "Zavattinian."

During the months spent at Zavattini's side, Giuseppe Bertolucci and Benigni were playing with the idea of a sequel to *Berlinguer ti voglio bene*. This was also because the Neapolitan producer Gianni Minervini was still very much convinced that Roberto was meant for the movies. "We considered the idea of a grown-up Pinocchio, a man about twenty-five, sort of vicious, but only in order to survive; a puppet without strings and kind of pissed off at everything." It was to be a transition between Cioni Mario and other new characters. All of Benigni's future films would aim in this direction, intended to overcome the extreme violence of that first screen release.

And in the meantime Roberto was on a steady diet of film classics, assiduously attending film-club evenings in Rome,

The Benigni-RAI relationship. It seems like the conjugation into infinity of the future of Benigni: I will Benigni, you will Benigni. I wanted to... I really liked to Benigni a lot, but they never let me Benigni very much at the RAI... it always turns out that I'll "Benigni-RAI" as they say in the future, you'll "Benigni-RAI"...

Roberto practices for his performance on Oscar night!

places such as the Film Studio, L'Occhio, l'orecchio, la bocca. He went to watch Chaplin, Harold Lloyd, and especially Buster Keaton. "I think he was the master from whom I borrowed most," he explained. "I admired him for his impassiveness, for those gags that were born out of the melancholy of just existing."

It was precisely during those days that Ugo Gregoretti offered him the role of the "thinker" in *Ma cos'è quest'amore* [But what is this love], a comedy by Achille Campanile broadcast on RAI 1. For RAI 2, Roberto appeared in a series of specials and shows, halfway between theatre and cabaret, directed by Luciano Michetti-Ricci, Fiorella Infascelli, Marco Melani (one of the founding fathers of the Roman film-club circuits).

During that same period Federico Fellini was thinking about using Benigni as an alternative to Mastroianni for the leading role in *City of Women* (*Città delle donne*, 1980), but Roberto's age presented a problem. In any case, big budget films were only interested in typecasting him as the venomous little imp.

In the late seventies Benigni appeared with some frequency, though in stories not his own. Many of these could not have been further from who he really was. He worked hard at trying to fit into characters with whom he had nothing in common. He lacked the versatility of the "professional," ready to assume any role to get the exposure.

He gave a mild performance in *Tigers in Lipstick* (*Letti selvaggi*, 1979), an episode film which marked the final decline of the old master of Italian comedy, Luigi Zampa. Bernardo Bertolucci came up with a little role for him, more out of affection than narrative necessity – and it showed – in his film *Luna* (*La Luna*, 1979), in which Benigni plays the clownish role of a bungling decorator. Once having worked as the barman at the Casa del Popolo of Vergaio, Roberto even played the barman in a big hotel in *Clair de femme* (1979), an unexpected incursion by Costantin Costa-Gavras into the territory of sentimental comedy. It had an all-star Italian-French-German cast and the "little devil" from Tuscany seemed to be right in his element. The year 1979 also witnessed the making of *I giorni cantati* [Singing days, 1979] a film directed by a singer-composer (Paolo Pietrangeli) and packed with singer-composers (such as Francesco Guccini, Ivan Della Mea, Giovanna Marini). And Roberto could not be kept from singing, executing some *lied* by Schubert together with Mariangela Melato.

But the filmmaker who succeeded in adapting Benigni's personality to a film script more than any other director during that period was Marco Ferreri. He offered Roberto the part of a

That would really be it if in dramatic films we didn't have fun, it is precisely tragic things that make us burst out laughing.

schoolteacher in *Chiedo asilo* [Looking for shelter, 1979] . For, just as Robin Williams, Roberto was also an actor who risked feeling cramped in films, his uncontainable vitality seemingly far removed from the expressive impoverishment of cinematic naturalism. Ferreri got Benigni's "excessive" histrionics to bear fruit by placing them in the proper context, that is, amidst the existential paradoxes of a group of children in a nursery school. Of course, nursery-school teacher Benigni resorted to all the devices of the imagination that, in any case, corresponded to an exalted and visionary version of the Montessori teaching method. He treated the children on an equal basis, yet without forcing them into the world of adults: it was he who transforms himself and becomes a child instead, like Tom Hanks had done in *Big* (1988) though without the magic. Teacher Benigni sleeps with the children, leaps out of cupboards at them, appears as a "pregnant man," goes to the bathroom in the same mini-toilets and, in the end, even gets the parents to join in, having them enter the world of children and experience the same sensations.

Forced to put himself on the same level as such young ones, his role in *Chiedo asilo* gave Benigni the perfect opportunity of letting off his own childish exuberance. The most moving scenes are those in which Roberto teams up with a maladjusted pupil, a child who refuses to eat or speak. It is this child, in fact, who takes the teacher by the hand on the beach when, in the Ferrerian ending of *Chiedo asilo*, the teacher-clown refuses the role of father and decides to go away, returning to the maternal womb of the sea, and walks into the waves to drown himself. Benigni, incoherent in the scope of ordinary films, was brilliant in this moral fable which revealed his very personal authenticity, a far cry from cinema's routine reconstruction of reality.

It was during that same period that Renzo Arbore, under whose protective wing Benigni had been launched into celebrity on the TV program *L'altra domenica*, also landed up on the film scene with his menagerie of crazy animals. The idea was to bring his "gang's" television success to the screen. This project resulted in three films: *Il Pap'occhio*, *Il resto del Pap'occhio*

In my opinion God is truly something erotic that laughs. This is a very profound concept. Eroticism and comedy, when they appear together, make something very poetic, divine, like Marilyn Monroe. And God is Marilyn Monroe, the perfect union between sex and comedy.

[The rest of Pap'occhio] (unreleased) and finally *F.F.S.S. ovvero Che mi hai portato a fare sopra Posillipo se non mi vuoi più bene?* [The National Railway or What did you bring me up to Posillipo to do if you don't love me anymore?, 1983].

Masters to Betray

Just like Juda, Benigni betrayed Master Arbore (for 30 telephone tokens, instead of 30 denarii), selling him out to the Pope's adversaries who want to sabotage the show and its "evangelical policy."

We see Roberto the hero of precious entra'actes and sketches, little jewels of moonlight comedy, as when he speaks with God (Luciano De Crescenzo) in the Sistine Chapel or else, all alone, as he goes wandering through the Raphael rooms and the Vatican galleries, coming out from a shower in a bathrobe and skullcap to enter the Ponitifice's apartments and sit on Karol "ole Wotlya's" great armchair. The best sequence of *Pap'occhio* was the one in which Benigni accidentally passes behind the window

Opposite: *D'Alema I love you! Roberto Benigni with then PDS Secretary Massimo D'Alema.*

In my opinion if God dies, he'll go to hell. When he gave the Tables to Moses, he was really mad about all the mess at Sodom and Gomorrah. So, in his rage he made a mistake, like someone who makes up laws too quickly, and he made up the capital sins without realizing that they were all his own vices. And that is how he invented Pride: for who could be prouder than someone who calls himself God?

from which the Pope gives his blessings. Taken for the Holy Father, he triggers a great ovation and so starts having fun passing back and forth again and again behind the window… Benigni's model was clearly Groucho Marx, who was keeping vigil over him like a patron saint, inspiring many famous sequences right up to those in *Son of the Pink Panther* (*Il figlio della pantera rosa*, 1993), when the Marx Brothers are explicitly cited. This happens in the hospital scene as Inspector Dreyfus is resting – so to speak – enveloped in casts. Clouseau Junior confuses the remote control of the automatic bed with the TV's (where a Marx Brothers' film is being shown) with disastrous consequences.

Compared to *Pap'occhio*, Benigni's appearances in *F.F.S.S. ovvero Che mi hai portato a fare sopra Posillipo se non mi vuoi più bene?* are much shorter. Here the idea was that Arbore and De Crescenzo gather up sheets of paper that fall into the street from Federico Fellini's apartment window and use them to make a film. Roberto gets a truly Fellinian role, that of the "Beige Sheik," an obvious spoof of Alberto Sordi's *The White Sheik* (*Lo sceicco bianco*, 1952) inventor of the mythic Arabian Sound, who together with a band of false bedouins comes out with his hit *Aiutati che Allah ti aiuta* [Allah helps those who help

themselves]. It was just a minor role, but proved prophetic, since it prefigured Benigni as a Fellini hero, as in fact did materialize a few years later in *Voices of the Moon*.

In the presence of Fellini, even the irreverent Benigni (seems impossible!) had to step down, put the brakes on his merry intrusiveness and get inside the part which master Federico had cut out for him: Ivo Salvini, a star-struck loony who wanders around the countryside listening to the voice of the moon. Part Pinocchio, part sad poet, in the style of Giacomo Leopardi. "He guided me like a good father," Benigni recalled, a few years later, talking of his experience with the great film director from Rimini.

"If we could all just be quiet, maybe we would understand," suggests the madman Ivo at the end of the film. And yet, "Beware of understanding, all you have to do is listen." Roberto defined his character a "pure Dostoyevskian," a lunatic who had very little in common with the other heroes of the Benigni bestiary. Fellini bent Benigni's childish, exuberantly joyous screen character, turning him into a melancholic jester in his own poetic testament. Ivo was one of the countless self-portraits Fellini left us, and this was his last, most mournfully clownish. Unusually docile, Roberto answered the call and, for the first time ever, demonstrated that he was capable of straight acting, restrained, without frills or sly looks. The exercise was good for him, it enriched his background as an actor and added yet another feather to the Tuscan actor's cap, but at the same time it also weakened him, for it gave us a bloodless Benigni, very distant from the adrenaline levels at which his genius usually took flight.

Though tenderly, and in all friendliness, Benigni was nevertheless an actor who managed to take over directors' worlds, his comrades-in-arms. This is what happened with Ferreri, Citti, Jarmusch and even Blake Edwards. *Voices of the Moon* was the only film in which he willingly let himself be molded, disappearing into the poetic universe of another person, lending his own intrusive body to the visionary autobiography of that monument of a filmmaker, the one and only Fellini.

Dying of Hunger, Starved for Love

As many social misfits, Benigni's heroes were often mixed up with prisons (and, in fact, is not the Nazi lager of *Life Is Beautiful* but the most atrocious of all prisons?). Indeed two of his films begin precisely in prison: *Il minestrone* and *Down by Law*, which, moreover, have been recognized as particularly penetrating performances by Roberto.

Il minestrone (a "long" version of which was broadcast on television in three episodes) was not only a tale filled with Pasolinian mystery, but it also gave rise to his encounter with Vincenzo Cerami, who would later play such an important role in refining and guiding Robert Benigni's talent. Vincenzo liberally wrote screen stories for him, even eventually winning an Oscar nomination for himself for the screenplay of *Life Is Beautiful*. Formed in the "Bertoluccian" circle (Giuseppe and Bernardo Bertolucci, Kim Arcalli, Gabriella Cristiani, Renato Tafuri, Gianni Amico, Fiorella Infascelli, Marco Melani, etc.), he learned how important it was to be able to tell the stories of Christ-like suffering and pain through the use of intense narrative colors, like pop-art. With Citti and Cerami, Benigni began to approach the magic of Pasolinian-inspired equilibriums: miraculous, more fragile but also sharper, more truly "Italian" and steeped in mystery. He added a new touch of kindness to his bursting energy, Benigni in *Il minestrone*, accompanied by the Pasolinian heroes Ninetto Davoli and Franco Citti, accomplishes a picaresque journey through time and history. Together the three men wander over Italy, passing from one parable to another, as in a poetic Michelin

Guide, searching for restaurants and inns to appease their appetites. But this is never possible. They are eternally famished, suffering from a colossal hunger that is insatiable – just as impossible to satisfy as Cioni Mario's sexual lust, or the sexual hunger of the other Tuscan hoodlums of *Berlinguer ti voglio bene*.

Davoli, Citti and Benigni land up in some pretty mysterious, sinister restaurants. In one of these bizarre places, armed waiters even read them the menu. There are Lucullan tables where they must overcome perilous ordeals before contenting their appetites. They are forbidden to have a meal, if only in their dreams, when the three starved men conjure up the "Spaghetti Olympics." And then there is the imaginary little inn called "At the Tapeworm," where phony meals are served up and their table companions are

A passionate kiss for Walter Veltroni, PDS Secretary.

Renzo Rossellini, explaining the paradoxical economic laws of filmmaking to me, that is, postmodern, showed how, in terms of funding by the Ministry, it was impossible to make a ten-minute film, the classic "one-reeler." At the Ministry of Entertainment, ten-minute films just hadn't been foreseen, nor ones of twenty-four hours for that matter. This was also because cinemas would only have paid twenty thousand lire a day for them. "We have a Benigni slapstick here to show with E.T., how much will you give us?" And they all answered. "twenty-thousand lire." And so, since by putting together lots of shorts you could come up with the length of a Ministry feature, that's when, quick as lightning, the idea was suddenly triggered…

left to wolf down only dirt. "Hunger cannot be measured," declares Benigni, "hunger is like the waves of the sea…"

Through Citti's intermediary, Roberto did his homework, studying the Pasolini of "La ricotta" (1963) and inserting what he learned into a comic panorama immersed in tragedy, which was the best and most noble vein of Benigni's expressive world. "Comedy," explained the little devil, "does not exist without tragedy; it goes right along with the philosophical law of the contradiction of opposites." And Benigni held up the example of Totò who, over the years, had become one of his tutelary deities: "To get a pearl like Totò you need centuries and centuries of tragedy, suffering, despair, hunger. Behind him you need people who have died, who have suffered with their guts […], hordes of people who have spit blood." Benigni called upon this combination of comedy and tragedy in *Life Is Beautiful*, which nevertheless leans more towards the pathos of Chaplin. But the contradiction of opposites also appeared in the gags of *The Monster*, where a Benigni character armed with good intentions, never stops brandishing knives, awls, electric saws and other instruments, terrorizing presumed victims in a climate of monster psychosis.

With *Il minestrone* Benigni finally began to find his own path to screen comedy, a route that did not pass through the rather gaudy humor of Italian comedy, but through the magical realism of Citti, through the Pasolinian intimations in Cerami's writing, through the mythical (and insatiable) needs of the sub-proletariat who used laughs in order to destroy, not for fun. His was an anarchic laughter aimed at wrecking established order, questioning institutions and, even when expressed in the form of kindness (as in *The Little Devil*), carried within itself the seeds of revolution. He is one of those people who needs to destroy, just like the slapstick comedians of silent films.

Benigni's debut as a film director came with *Tu mi turbi* [You trouble me, 1983], an episode film written with Giuseppe Bertolucci and which came about when another idea fell through: that is, to shoot a series of shorts for Gaumont to be screened together with main feature films, as in the old days of comedy fillers. It was planned to have a *Benigni pompiere* [Benigni the fireman], a *Benigni sulla scala mobile* [Benigni on the escalator], a *Benigni e il diavolo* [Benigni and the devil], etc.

Tu mi turbi, which at first was to be entitled *Benigni a mezzanotte* [Benigni at midnight], was eventually produced by Ettore Rosboch. The film reflected a simple motion-picture model, polished but effective, dramatically reduced to the bone, in which director Benigni always chose the most crystal-clear solutions, without ever renouncing, however, his stamp as director (contrary to *Non ci resta che piangere* [All we can do is cry, 1984], where the

Opposite: *Roberto in the film* Non ci resta che piangere.

co-existence of two personalities as dissonant as Troisi's and Benigni's blocked the expression of one well-defined style).

The four short tales of *Tu mi turbi* are just as many monologues in disguise, each enriched with the presence of supporting players in the roles of classic straight men. In the episode "Durante Cristo" ["During Christ"] Benigni is a shepherd who, having lost all his sheep (except one, named "Lost"), is hired as a babysitter to look after little Jesus.

At first the child seems to be like any other, but of course he is in fact "very special." This gives the kick off for a new reading of the evangelical text and a chain of delightful sacrilegious gags (when the little one dries his face, he leaves his own image imprinted on the cloth, just like the Holy Shroud), but it also turns Roberto Benigni to reflect upon the universe of the divine. The episode "Angelo" ["Angel"], which is the loveliest, witnesses Benigni in the role of a guardian angel – with "such a lot of wings" – who has abandoned his "charge" because he is so boring. The sketch "In banca" ["At the bank"] on the other hand, a study of paradoxes, is also an act of accusation against the logic of the banking system, which lends money only to the wealthy: a poor man with no property goes out looking for a loan but receives only long meaningless speeches from these banks on the solvability of their other clients. The subject of "banking" exalts Benigni, particularly with his Marxist ideological background, and really brings out his claws (making him almost as lacerating as in his live performances), spurred by the naive anger of Totò and the lunatic indignation of Groucho Marx. "If I had a billion, would you give me a hundred million? Well then, I'll give you three hundred million, since I'll still have seven hundred left…"

The anarchic radicalism of this ideology is like a second skin: Benigni, as he himself explains, is a leftist down to the marrow in his bones and views the logic of capitalism with the same innocent wonder as a child or a Buster Keaton. The entire "adult" and middle-class world (people who have their heads on their shoulders) seems absurd to him. Just as absurd as the old myths of the military's sacrosanctity, put in the pillory in the final episode of *Tu mi turbi*, entitled "I militi" ["Soldiers"], where Benigni and his comrade-in-arms Claudio Bigagli spend the

night on guard at attention before the Tomb of the Unknown Soldier. Stone by stone, Benigni dismantles the edifice of ideological certitude upon which the military rite is founded, takes its gestures and habits out of context and eventually serves them up in all their nakedness, as in themselves incredibly ridiculous and meaningless.

Benigni's first directing effort is still perhaps one of his best. In *Tu mi turbi* he moved with the serenity of someone who had nothing to prove and directed his actors (only a few, and therefore easily manageable) with naturalness and good sense. The episodic structure of the film, moreover, gave him the opportunity of skipping from Child Jesus to the banking system, from guardian angels to the Unknown Soldier, without diluting his flashes of genius in a long story, and also without being forced to resolve complex dramatic problems.

To the drama of poetic cinema he preferred the lightness of the picaresque tale, such as in his *Il minestrone*. Like many comics, Benigni had the stamina of a hundred-meter (or at the very best, four-hundred-meter) sprinter, with less endurance in long-distance

The thing that gave me the most pleasure in directing was being able to give orders, something that had never happened to me before. With Ferreri, when at seven in the morning he would say to me, "Let's go!" I used to say to myself, "If I were the director, I wouldn't say to myself, 'Let's go.'" And I didn't. We always started at three in the afternoon, and we still didn't even go over by one day. I had planned to film practically all night, in order to have the same working hours as the theatre.

competitions (and indeed even the so highly acclaimed *Life Is Beautiful* seems to be divided into two very funny stumps, practically a diptych made up of two separate films: the first part, set in Italy, has the bright, pretty tones of a realistic Zavattinian comedy; the second, set in Germany, in the concentration camp, presents the gloomy and unreal hues of a nightmare, a theatrical kammerspiel).

We again come across the picaresque structure in the film-for-four-hands, *Non ci resta che piangere*, a project which saw the light particularly thanks to the good business flair of producer Troisi Mauro Berardi and also Benigni's then guardian angel Ettore Rosboch. While peacefully traveling along a country road, schoolteacher Benigni and his buddy Troisi find themselves, no one knows how, in Frittole, in Tuscany, in the year 1492. This crazy trip back in time plunges them right in the midst of the violent clashes between disciples and opponents of Savonarola. Dragged despite themselves into bloody family feuds, terrified at the idea of not being able to return to the twentieth century, our two heroes are invited to stay at Vitellozzo's estate (the indispensable Carlo Monni), who offers them new clothes and oversees their education. In the end, Benigni and Troisi set off to explore the world of the 1400s.

Non ci resta che piangere is an elementary-school primer that gathers together fragmentary sketches on medieval and renaissance history and literature. Some successfully, others less so. Roberto willingly played the supporting player for Troisi here and there, particularly in shared sentimental situations, such as the serenade scene to Amanda Sandrelli. This comes closer to the light cabaret of the Smorfia than the cosmic pessimism of Cioni Mario. The meeting with Leonardo da Vinci is revealing: the two propose to go into business with him, intending to profit from patents on future inventions. Unfortunately though, this Leonardo is almost a complete idiot… Though written and executed by both Troisi and Benigni, *Non ci resta che piangere* belonged more to the light vein of early Troisi than to Benigni's magical world. Moreover, the narrative flow that twists and turns recalls the brusque stops and starts of Troisi's comedy rather than the crystalline structures of Benigni's films.

> *I can't stand the film-editing machine. No matter how wonderful everyone says it is, I don't believe it. I liked editing, though, because it gave me the same feeling as when we were kids and used to do cut-out albums, figures that could first be stuck and then unstuck. But editing is also deathly, a torture without end, something that killed me. Once Ferreri said to me that editing was a film's breath, but breathing like that is like opening a cylinder of gas.*

To rescue their friend Vitellozzo, the two write a letter to Savonarola, obviously a take-off on Totò and Peppino De Filippo's famous letter they dictate in the cult movie *Totò, Peppino e… la malafemmina* [Totò, Peppino and… the femme fatale, 1956]

Like a little spirit, Benigni follows his travelmate Troisi in amazement as the latter blatantly robs songs from Modugno and the Beatles. And, like the post-peasant Tuscany of Cioni Mario, this fifteenth-century world also has its excremental soul (chamber pots emptied out the window), though they are now reduced to simple caricature.

More in the Benigni style is the anarchist project to keep Christopher Columbus from discovering America and therefore making sure the world does not fall under the cultural and economic domination of the United States (perhaps the Academy's members might not have been amused…). But Troisi and Benigni get to the port too late, when the ships have already sailed, due to an error in the departure date in master Benigni's history book. *Non ci resta che piangere* offered the creative merriment of these various episodes, but lacked that poetic and magical quality that makes *Tu mi turbi* so special.

Roberto with little Giorgio Cantarini on the set of Life Is Beautiful.

GIVE MY LOVE TO HOLLYWOOD

If master Saverio (Benigni) and his buddy Mario (Troisi) ever did manage to stop Christopher Columbus from sailing off with his three ships, not even Cioni Mario would ever have made it to Hollywood.

The America that Benigni first came into contact with professionally, as that little mischievous movie imp, was the America of Walter Matthau, Blake Edwards, and above all, Jim Jarmusch. These were people who were little concerned (if at all) by the standards or moods of Hollywood. *His* America was most of all Jarmusch, with whom he made *Down by Law*, the short subject *Coffee and Cigarettes* (1986), the Roman episode of *Night on Earth* (1992), and to whom he owed Nicoletta Braschi's participation in *Mystery Train* (1989).

Paths crossed for Jarmusch and Benigni in 1984 in Salsomaggiore, where both were on the Jury of the Salso Film & TV Festival (created by Marco Melani, once Benigni's director for television). Two years later Jarmusch had the crazy idea of involving him in a film to be shot in the swamps of Louisiana and Benigni, the just as crazy idea to accept. How they would

I had always dreamed of not going to America. Every so often I would say to myself, "One day or other I won't go to America." But instead, I did.

ever be able to even understand each other only God knew. Benigni did not speak a word of English, Jarmusch not a word of Italian. Nevertheless, Jarmusch's filmmaking was a Wenders-like cinema, open to provocation, made up of minimalist journeys and emotions, very far removed from the drama of naturalist film. And so, miraculously, they clicked. In fact, their collaboration worked our far better than the "new comedy team" Benigni-Troisi, which was rather energetically banal.

The little devil of Vergaio brought to *Down by law* (in black and white photography by the Wendersian Robbie Muller, who later did the cinematography for *The Little Devil*) all of his destructive charge – as well as his now inseparable Nicoletta Braschi, who here too played his "princess." Benigni offered to the film a creative input – just as he had done in the *Son of the Pink Panther* – far beyond the call of an actor's participation. Benigni is by definition intrusive (he even went so far as to give the film his own Italian title, *Daunbailò*), but Jarmusch succeeded in getting all of this Benigni-energy to bear fruit.

Three convicts are thrown together in the same cell of a stinking prison: a down-and-out disc jockey (the singer Tom Waits), a pimp (John Lurie, saxophonist of the Lounge Lizards and Evan Lurie's brother who later composed the musical score for *The Little Devil*), and the gleefully hysterical Italian dreamer who has nothing of a criminal about him except for being guilty of having killed a man by hitting him on the forehead with a billiard ball (an affectionate tribute to fellow countryman Francesco Nuti?).

Roberto with Paolo Bonacelli in Taxisti di notte *di Jim Jarmusch.*

Benigni acted in a halting but very funny English, alternating beginners' rote expressions ("What a lovely day!") with recycled tongue twisters in Italian, taking up a piece of chalk to draw windows on the walls and infect his cellmates with his energy. After their escape, the three convicts end up trekking across the swamps of Louisiana. Roberto catches a rabbit and cooks it according to Mamma Isolina's recipe. Jarmusch left space for Roberto's autobiographical vein – taking off on that roast rabbit – and slipped in the flavors of the old house in Vergaio and all of Roberto's family, including his sisters, into the dialogue of *Down by Law*. And then came the good fairy Nicoletta, an almost Disney-like Snow White, with whom our hero sets up house in a little cottage in the woods, as he waves goodbye to his fellow fugitives.

Less inspired was the episode "Roma" in the film *Night on Earth*, where the gabby taxi driver Benigni limits himself to recycling one of his monologues, a long sexual outburst in the style of Cioni Mario (carousing with pumpkins and sheep and a sister-in-law who "gets it from the back," etc.) and gives one of his passengers a heart attack, the scrupulous prelate Paolo Bonacelli.

The idea of bringing back the adventures of inspector Clouseau with all of Benigni's physical frenzy, turned out to be excellent (thanks to Aurelio De Laurentiis, who launched the project). In many ways *Son of the Pink Panther*, the eighth film in the Pink Panther series, seemed just perfect. Directed by Blake Edwards in his own style and enriched by Benigni's physical exuberance, Roberto did not let himself be intimidated by the great master (nor why should he have been, when he had already acted under Fellini?), nor the burdensome inheritance of Peter Sellers. The film began with second-class gendarme Jacques Gambrelli and his very Italian mamma Claudia Cardinale who reveals to the amazed Herbert Lom that the big bungler in uniform is none other than Clouseau's son. Really him. And there we have detective Clouseau Junior following in his father's footsteps, without forgetting any of his allies, enemies, nor even the legendary disguises. Some of the sequences are hilarious with phenomenal gags. Absolutely not to be missed is a slapstick chase scene in the purest tradition of Mack Sennett's silent comedies, as Roberto, on a most unfortunate Velosolex motor bike, drives into potholes, subway excavations, between tramlines, on the verge of constant disaster. Herbert Lom, with all the weight of his years, puts up with Clouseau Junior's misadventures with resignation, literally tormented by him and his involuntary sadism, punctuated by a crescendo of gags, that grow crueler and crueler, and more and more contorted by the minute. When the poor Lom is finally plastered up like a mummy in the hospital, with his multiple fractured limbs in traction, the remote control for his bed ends up in Benigni's hands and this becomes irresistible. The hospital's innovative equipment turns into an instrument of torture. And Clouseau Junior winds up watering daisies growing out of Herbert Lom's foot cast.

Son of the Pink Panther would have been an absolute jewel had

Roberto is also a poet. I still have all the little verses he left for me every morning on the set.
WALTER MATTHAU, ACTOR

it not been for the dubbing. Indeed, the film was shot in English and Benigni dubbed himself in Italian, but with horrible results. Perhaps this was because he lacked the lip precision of a professional dubber (all of his lines are terribly out of sync), or because, with the process of dubbing in the way, everything became a little like warmed up soup and his acting lost that great immediacy which is one of his strongest qualities. Truly a shame!

Whatever the case may be, the most miraculous marriage between Benigni and America was brought about by an all-Italian film, *The Little Devil*, which was an experience much the same, yet quite the opposite of *Down by Law*. This time it was an Italian director (Benigni himself) who was offering a part in a film that could not be more "Made in Italy" to an actor who could not be more "Made in USA," that is, Walter Matthau.

Matthau played don Maurizio, a priest in crisis and, to make matters worse, in love with Stefania Sandrelli. An expert exorcist, he manages to expel, out of the possessed body of a chubby female, the little devil named Giuditta (just like Roberto's real aunt's name who saved him as a child from drowning in the cesspool). Very soon the little devil becomes as attached to the priest as a stray pup, following him everywhere, imitating his every move, making him excruciatingly self-conscious. Matthau, as everyone knows, is rarely surprised at anything, very much like Buster Keaton. But having this childish pest of a demon underfoot drives the irritable exorcist priest up the wall. Matthau's imperturbable countenance mirrors all the equally crazy things the little devil Benigni gets

With Walter Matthau in The Little Devil.

In jail in Jim Jarmusch's Down by Law.

up to. But soon the priest becomes almost protective towards him, like master Geppetto and the naughty Pinocchio.

Though eerily invisible to any mirrors, the devil Giuditta is much less demoniacal than the lost souls of *Berlinguer ti voglio bene*. As a character, he embodies the last memories of Cioni Mario's earthly devilry, the last attempts at obscenities, animalistic thrusts, rampant excitation of the senses, puns set against a crudely sexual backdrop. One of the film's dialogues, in a restaurant scene amidst priests and Messeigneurs, plays on the ambiguity between diabolical possession and physical possession, where the little devil Benigni, shocking a prelate, risks giving him a heart attack just as he did Paolo Bonacelli in *Night on Earth*.

But *The Little Devil* already had the splendid magic of the

I believe in God. I'm someone who is constantly in contact with the devil, and so, what I mean is that I'm also involved with the opposite side — that there's a dialogue, dialectics.

pure comic Benigni who had renounced his destructive mission in order to enjoy (and have us enjoy) the geometric progressions of those ambiguities and gags of which he is a masterful interpreter. Giuditta already had the tenderness of his more recent characterizations which, with Chaplin-like astuteness, were aimed at winning the hearts of the public. Giuditta is a wee little devil who is "born" into our world – a world which is in fact much more senseless and cruel than Hell could ever be. The little devil is as naked as a baby, as tender as a stuffed panda, as devoid of any of the "social defenses" adults are armed with, beginning with language: Giuditta repeats everything, meaninglessly, picking up the first words he hears (the running gag was: "I'm Gloria. I left my driver's license on the table next to the fruit bowl.") completely out of context, and which created an absolutely hilarious effect.

Benigni in *The Little Devil* is all fun and innocence. He even treats his favorite subject, sex, with a light touch. The discovery of woman and femininity, again embodied by Nicoletta Braschi (who gives an excellent performance here in the role of a graceful and charming woman), is like a game. The little devil Giuditta puts Nina on his shoulders and lets her ride him like a horse, feeling "that little thing that men don't have" up against his neck. In the end he discovers that Nina is a devil just like he is, sent to Earth to take him back by the most wonderful means of transportation that exists: love.

Evil is never so dangerously interwoven with love as in *The Little Devil*: little devilish Pinocchios, gentle she-devils, exorcists in love, scandalized priests. Benigni, who had already brought to the screen bored guardian angels (with "such a lot of wings!"), here in joyous sacrilege brews a mixture of the profane with the most turbid figures of Catholic religiosity. The result is the subtlest of films, as light as a whisper, whose characters, despite being uplifted by the wind, obviously prefer to remain rooted to the material world.

Roberto Benigni, Nicoletta Braschi, Tom Waits and John Lurie in Down by Law *directed by Jim Jarmusch.*

Robertino and the Wolf

Yes, being in films was wonderful, but where was the audience? Every so often Roberto felt the desperate need to re-establish contact with a flesh-and-blood public, with real people who shouted, applauded, screamed, laughed. And so he had his manager Vincenzo Ratti organize a show. "I felt the need to just lay down over the people, to smell them, touch them, feel their flesh." Live entertainment brought him back to life. Working as an actor for someone like Fellini in a film such as *Voices of the Moon* (a very long process, interminable, as work always was on Fellini's films) had exhausted him, drained him of his real energy, which came from his contact with people. In the fall of 1989 Ermanno Olmi had a project for a film ready that could possibly involve Benigni and his beloved Nicoletta. But there was another real surprise waiting: Robert Altman, who had come to Italy to shoot a film on the life of Rossini at Cinecittà, wanted

him for the role of the famous composer. If there was anyone who could portray the torrential energy which was the driving force of Rossini's music, it was certainly Benigni. But the Rossini project bogged down, a new producer came on the scene, Altman handed over the direction to Monicelli and the project was revamped. Benigni was out. And even the project with Olmi went up in smoke. Roberto was happy to be able to devote himself to his stage tours, to the physical contact with the public. "People," he said, "react differently to a comic than to an actor or a singer. When they see me, they touch me, joke with me, kick me in the ass, touch my genitals…"

The most unbelievable performance ever for Roberto Benigni took place on 12 November 1990. It was the day he appeared as an actor on the stage of an opera house for the very first time. This was not going to be any of the usual furious theatre-cabaret monologues punctuated by super-curses or fecal indigestion, but rather a real concert production, with a real orchestra there, in the Town Hall of Ferrara, with the world-famous orchestra conductor Claudio Abbado directing the Chamber Orchestra of Europe. Music by Mozart, Berio, Stroppa and Prokofiev.

Roberto Benigni, with hair well-combed and nicely dressed (it did happen once in a while), looked absolutely impeccable among the impeccable orchestra maestros as he made his way to the podium: it would be Roberto to recite the voice part of Prokofiev's symphonic fairy tale, *Peter and the Wolf*, a work which had taught generations of good middle-class children to distinguish between the sounds of the various musical instruments.

The role, in the past, had been entrusted to Gérard Philippe and to Eduardo De Filippo, in other words, to more "serious" actors than Benigni. To see him in a tuxedo was already a show in itself. The tickets sold out fast and many people were left disappointed outside the theatre. Inside, instead of the usual concert crowd there were lots of people from the film world, producers (Vittorio Cecchi Gori and Carlo Ponti), directors (his

faithful buddy Giuseppe Bertolucci), actors (Paolo Villaggio). There was the then Minister of Entertainment, the Socialist Carlo Tognoli. The public listened attentively to Roberto's performance, hailed him, called him back loudly for an encore… and this was when he really took off, performing as an encore his own extravagant and completely personal ending to the fairy tale, turning the one written by Prokofiev inside out. "We here at the Chamber Orchestra have discovered something…" trilled Peter-Benigni with that devilish look in his eyes. And, in the Benignian version, in the end the cat eats the little bird and the hunters the duck, while the grumpy Grandad gets sent to the zoo.

But those who had seen the concert's dress rehearsals reported that they had been even more hilarious, with Benigni getting the cat and the wolf all mixed up, deliberately setting the lines topsy turvy and waiting for Abbado to scold him, moving his arms like the blades of a windmill, making faces at topical parts of the tale. For his part, Abbado made superhuman efforts to keep a straight face and maintain the decorum expected of an orchestra conductor. To everyone's amazement, Cioni Mario abandoned his anarchic obscenities and adopted culture with a capital "C" with his dark suit of exclusive soirées. At the press conference Benigni had fun teasing them all and threatened: "Pavarotti watch out! I'll soon be singing Rossini…" probably alluding to Altman's Rossini film project.

A short while after this performance, Roberto appeared in a historic *Lectura Dantis* at the University of Siena, where he had been invited to participate in the University's 750th anniversary. To receive him there was the rector Luigi Berlinguer, in whose presence Roberto avoided talking about himself, reverting to the title of his old film *Berlinguer ti voglio bene*. This Berlinguer bestowed upon Roberto the *honoris causa* degree in Theatre Sciences and Literature as the audience, with stadium-like enthusiasm, ranted "Kiss! Kiss!" And in the end, Benigni did plant a big kiss (academic or not) on rector Berlinguer's nose, the Minister of Education-to-be under Italy's future left-wing government. Dante had always been his passion. Roberto added a little showmanship to the Great Poet's masterpiece,

Left: Pinocchio show, a children's favorite.

Left: *Roberto Benigni and Paolo Villaggio in Federico Fellini's* Voices of the Moon. *Opposite: Benigni and Villaggio.*

contaminating the *Divine Comedy* with reflections on current issues. Moreover, if Craxi had lived in Dante's time, wouldn't he also have been relegated to some great Circle of Hell?

The students listened enthralled while Roberto set about brushing off centuries of dust from the Great Poet's icon, making him incredibly immediate, "pleasurable," as he liked to say. "The Divine Comedy is so clear and simple," he explained, "it's just that sometimes the notes are difficult. And then, you always love Dante. In short, as everyone knows, you go home, grind the coffee, and every so often take a peek at *The Divine Comedy*. And then as for me, from where I'm from, I lived and breathed Dante. My mother and my uncle Attilio constantly talked about Dante." In the Circle of the Lustful, Benigni really had something to get his teeth into. "It's the Circle with the least suffering of any of them. It's the one with Semiramis, who was really a big pig. He was such a pig that he passed an edict declaring that all his subjects had to act like pigs. That way, he felt normal." Although he purposely went fishing in troubled waters, Roberto still had boundless respect for Dante, in his own way, of course. Thus he stressed what he defined as "Dante's sensuality," since, "if you're going to last 700 years you need to be pretty erotic. And in real life too Dante liked women, he had seven or eight children. In short, he was what in Tuscany you would call a real fucker, in the highest sense of the word. And – wouldn't you know it – the most populated Circle of Hell is the one of the Lustful."

As for myself, I prefer not to read The Divine Comedy, *but rather to recite it by heart. Dante is easy to learn, you read him once and he stays in your head, in fact, there are even tercets that you read and just can't stop hearing, like a little refrain.*

Gag Thieves

It was during the film *The Little Devil* that Benigni and writer Vincenzo Cerami grew close, someone who in later years became his most assiduous confrère, replacing Giuseppe Bertolucci, who had weaned and guided Roberto in the early years of his career. Cerami left his mark on Benigni's films, just as Bertolucci had before him. Contrary to other comics of

I have known Cerami for many, many years and he has really taught me so many things. How can I show you ? With his style. Let me describe him: he's of average height, rugged looking, a compulsive eater (he can come in and devour a roll of Scottex without even saying hello), oozing with meanness that only dissipates when you look him in the eyes, an extremely difficult thing to do, but once you do, you discover an oriental saffron color that soothes both body and soul. He's so shy he can melt right into a carpet, very erotic when he dances rock, he's another one of us who lives and sleeps with the moon, in a waking dream that he has lived since eternity. He loves women, but really a lot, such a lot, he is truly consumed by the madness, but in vain does he knock at poetry's door, which is its own master.

Left and opposite: *Roberto in one of his live shows.*

the generation (if we consider the vain Francesco Nuti), Benigni had enough modesty to let himself be guided, and had quite a good flair for choosing the people who could truly enrich him with new material. When appropriate, he knew how to be just like clay in the hands of his screenwriters. And the results speak for themselves.

His chemistry with the expressive world of Cerami (who would later receive an Oscar nomination for his screenplay of *Life Is Beautiful*) was perfect, even if very soon it began to strike out in new directions, turning towards the refined and delicate structures of pure comedy. In Cerami's hands, Benigni grew more and more to resemble Charlie Chaplin, on the one hand using gags as an important device, and on the other, expressing strong emotional content. His collaboration with Cerami gave birth to *Johnny Stecchino* (1991), a film structured in the pure tradition of incongruous comedy where Benigni plays a double role: the good guy and the bad, just like Chaplin in *The Great Dictator* (1952). On the one hand, he was the boss Johnny, tracked by enemies and the police, forced to live as a perpetual fugitive; and on the other hand, he was his double, Dante, a well-meaning man who accompanies disabled children to school and only has one little "vice," when he steals bananas from the fruit stall.

The entire film is constructed upon these hilarious banana gags (and on three or four other comic finds) and might be criticized as rather lacking in content. Through the whole story, the good Dante, who ends up in the most terrible messes, is convinced that all of his problems stem from a stolen banana and he cannot possibly understand how one little banana could be of such vital interest to the police, to everyone around him, to criminals. The irony is not an end in itself, but is a jibe at the

Whatever can't stand up to ridicule is due to collapse. However, whatever can't take seriousness is also going to collapse. Therefore, ridicule and seriousness are one and the same. So, if a system can be dismantled with ridicule, it can also be dismantled with tragedy. Consequently, let's say that tragedy dismantles the system, and ridicule, which is the same thing as tragedy, dismantles the system.

famous paradoxes of the legal system: one stolen banana can bring down the law in all its iron-clad severity, yet for the embezzlement of millions of dollars everything can be hushed up and come to nothing. In short, two years in prison for someone who steals a banana, but a Hawaiian paradise for someone who has gone conveniently "bankrupt." All of Benigni's gags continued to have a left-wing ideological backdrop, also thanks to Cerami's influence: the cultural humus of the new Benigni remained rooted in "Red" Tuscany, the one of cooperatives and "Case del Popolo." This was true not only of his comic monologues, in which the opportunism of the Craxian Italian middle class was his target, but also of the Christmas films produced by Cecchi Gori, and right up to his public readings of the verses of *The Divine Comedy*.

Another hilarious gag that ran throughout the entire narrative of *Johnny Stecchino* was the theme of cocaine. The killer Paolo Bonacelli (Benigni tries to use him like a Walter Matthau, with his deadpan Buster Keaton look) gets the good Dante to believe that this white powder is an "American" medicine against diabetes, and Dante – with his inevitable destructive innocence – publicly unmasks a prefect who sniffs non-stop.

Benigni recounted the Sicily of the Mafia with a touch of lightness, though never actually mentioning the word ever and, above all, without ever slipping into the banality seen in so many films. In this way he anticipated the miraculous balance achieved by *Tano da morire* [Tano to die, 1997], Roberta Torre's first feature-length film, and whose title was a play on the typical Sicilian name "Tano" and the expression, "I love you to death." It tells the story, far from the commonplaces of cinema and television, of Sicilian organized crime, managing, as does *Johnny Stecchino*, to treat the culture of the Mafia in a "light," though no less authentic way. It seems that Benigni had fun demystifying taboos

through films which took on subjects normally considered "things you don't joke about."

In *Johnny Stecchino* the strategic weight attributed to his (beloved) female consort Nicoletta Braschi took on an even greater importance and, indeed, film after film she was becoming a true co-star in all of Benigni's motion-picture adventures. Unlike *The Little Devil*, Matthau was no longer there to team up with Roberto, since Braschi herself was the fulcrum of the story, the link between the two characters (the bad *Johnny Stecchino* and his good double Dante).

As Fulvio Wetzl points out in his essay "The Divine Rascal," it was Johnny Stecchino himself who was "the manifesto of the new Benigni plan, intended to build gag upon gag without any reference to reality, for the sole purpose of making people laugh." To achieve this, his characters became increasingly more

scatterbrained, more and more inclined to dreaming, ever more glaringly distant from the reality in which they were plunged, more childishly victim to a world dominated by incomprehensible laws, just as Guido Orefice would be in *Life Is Beautiful*.

This was also the case of *The Monster*, a film in which Benigni portrayed a down-and-out Chaplin-like character. Loris was today's version of the Chaplin vagabond "tramp" who, brought up to date, became an unemployed anti-hero, living a hand-to-mouth existence as he filched at the supermarket and waited for a remote (nothing could be more unlikely) possibility of being hired by a surreal company with its head office located, no less, in Peking, China.

It was not by chance that the presumed 'monster' of *The Monster* happened to be jobless. In Italy, just as people everywhere were declaring the great economic boom, the ranks of the country's unemployed were quickly swelling beneath the surface of this apparent well-being. Cerami and Benigni put together a fairy tale – mid-way between Zavattini and Pasolini – in which society's rejection of the unemployed merged tendentiously with its terror of "the monster." The jobless man was likened to a monster. The bitter paradox of the film was to be found precisely in this statement, hidden within a Christmas comedy destined to rake in millions of dollars at the box office (in the end, it would bring home more than 50, an indisputable box-office record for the 1994-95 season). The same social diversity afflicts both the jobless man as well as the monster: the latter, the horror provoked by the crimes committed by the monster; the former, the middle-class horror caused by anyone who cannot "consume." Whoever does not participate in society's great consumer banquet is a potential monster…

But who was this "monster" anyway? In the mid-eighties the "monster of Florence" appeared almost daily in the front-page headlines of all Italian newspapers. These were the years filled with sex-related crimes attributed to the Tuscan serial killer

Left: *Gala evening with Benigni, Mario Cecchi Gori and Paolo Villaggio.*
Right: *Insolent and suspicious in* Johnny Stecchino.

Above: *Roberto and Debrah Farentino in a scene from* Son of the Pink Panther.
Opposite: *Roberto and the 'Pink Panther'.*

Pacciani, a man who came from those very same hills that had given birth to the hoodlums of *Berlinguer ti voglio bene*. Italy was living at the height of a monster psychosis to the point that even an inoffensive guy like Benigni might seem suspicious… And there was poor Loris fleeing along the desolate sidewalks of Rome's outskirts, pursued by a crowd gone insane (but without violence, like a Zavattini tale), men who wanted to take the law into their own hands against a slapstick character, fluttering his eyes as if in a Mack Sennett silent movie.

Criminologists and the police hunt down Loris, the good guy, who once again (as in *Johnny Stecchino*) has been confused with a bad guy. Benigni was aiming at a comedy of the equivocal. All of his films from this point on would be directed to this purpose (as would the Jew Guido Orefice when he conceals the horrors of the Holocaust from the eyes of his little boy). In *The Monster* a thousand fortuitous circumstances fan the fires of the equivocal, and most of all a well-contrived rebellion of objects: big knives, awls, electric saws, quite ordinary tools and utensils that plot to undermine the hero's claim to innocence, as he is "discovered" time and again brandishing these arms with equivocal rage. The capacity to develop an estranged use of the objects – something also typical of silent movies – represents one of the strengths of the film, just as the estranged use of words is in *The Little Devil*. Moreover, the policewoman Jessica (Nicoletta Braschi, of course) shadows the presumed "monster" Loris and, in an effort to surprise him in the act, tries to provoke him with an endless chain of sexual propositions to which the hero – an inside gag – remains insensitive. The sexual lust of Cioni Mario resurfaces only to make him a laughing-stock. *The Monster* is filled with self-directed irony, written with great inventive richness, deeply steeped (as is the case traditionally in cabaret) in current events. Benigni snowballs gag after gag with obvious amusement, to the point of even over doing it. The obsessive vitality of the presumed "monster" fits the little devil's energy perfectly. It is a film too obviously written for Benigni and which no one else could have ever acted, if not a Chaplin brought back to life, a Keaton, or at best perhaps a Robin Williams. The comic devices are studied and resolved with split-second precision, though the overall impact is not equal to all of them as a whole, nor is the directing, in the noblest sense of the word. *The Monster* is one of those very funny films in which – as sometimes happens to Benigni as director – long lapses are evident where the director seems to have dropped out of his role, as if he is somewhere else, perhaps too busy working on his character.

Certain sequences that seem resolved with excessive lightness give us the strong sensation that Benigni, like Keaton, might have needed a co-director capable of overseeing the mise en scène. But in fact this would have been impossible, since

Benigni's comedy – despite the fact that it is based on the devices of the gag – moves in the domain of the auteur. It is in fact from this point of view that *The Monster* remains one of his less successful films, since it is pure device, without that gentleness of touch which inspires the films *Tu mi turbi* or *The Little Devil*.

All of Benigni's films (*The Monster* in particular), are overly Benigni-centric and show a number of oversights in the directing, in the bit characters, in the setting. His screen model is marked, even in its best moments, with a certain air of the theatre, of the stage, of the wings: a "one-man-show" which swells into a filmic tale yet keeps something of its non-cinematic origins.

Nevertheless, this apparent technical negligence in the directing is still not too troublesome since Giuseppe Bertolucci, in the beginning, and Vincenzo Cerami afterwards, constructed for Benigni (and with Benigni) a narrative universe that appealed to the fairy tale, to the moral fable, that journeyed in a direction in

which the realism of a "strong" cinematic structure, in the round, might even have been troublesome. Benigni's cinema is merrily two-dimensional: it never pretends to be real. Thus the lack of three-dimensionality in the mise en scène works very well. In his films we never find complicated camera movements or a refined use of depth of field. Like Chaplin, Benigni needs a linear filmic language, he needs frontal vision, the solidarity of a "friendly" camera, close and fixed. Only in this way can he contrive his verbal and psychological balancing acts.

For that matter Benigni, unlike other comics of this generation also committed to one-man-shows, never slips into self-indulgence, since as a tightrope walker of punch lines and improvisation (like Totò was), he has acquired a miraculous sense of measure.

Nicoletta, My Love

Gentle, defenseless, teary eyed, soft-spoken and slightly mischievous, Nicoletta Braschi is the moving Edna Purviance of Roberto (Chaplin) Benigni, his Paulette Godard, wife and muse.

Nicoletta's first "Benignesque" appearance dates back to the episode "Durante Cristo" of *Tu mi turbi*, in which she portrayed the Virgin Mary, the wife of carpenter Carlo Monni, desired by the shepherd Benigni, who even then did not hide that he was very deeply in love with her. In fact Nicoletta was hanging on her Prince Charming's every word from the days of his first stage appearances as Cioni Mario: someone still remembers her at the doors of the Teatro Alberichino in Roma, waiting to catch sight of Roberto.

Their love story is a long and tender one, on the set as well as off. On the screen he courted her, loved her, carried her horseback, put her on his shoulders, won her over from much higher placed men, declared the fatal "I want to make love to you," and married her. Above all, her beloved Roberto included her in the cast of almost all his films, even in some of those in which he acted only, such as *Down by Law* or *Son of the Pink*

Roberto with his beloved Nicoletta on the set of Johnny Stecchino.

"launched" in style by her beloved Roberto, she had played a supporting female role in *Come sono buoni i bianchi* [How good the whites are, 1988] by Marco Ferreri (a director and friend of Benigni's, with whom he had already made *Chiedo asilo*). Beyond all other considerations it should be emphasized that Nicoletta (her voice, her gentleness, her child-like beauty, and even her theatrical bearing) creates perfect chemistry with Benigni's predilection for the fairy tale, with his desire to portray a moral fable at all costs, against any realism.

Almost always cast as a schoolteacher, Nicoletta, who often acts above the lines, like a theatrical doll, is the ideal support for Roberto's sentimental leaps and bounds, which have become, with the passing of the years, increasingly more gentle and childish, less and less sexual.

One might say that it was in fact Nicoletta (as well as Cerami's influence and the necessity to reach a vaster and less ideologically marked audience) to gradually soften the more archaic and bestial peasant instincts of Cioni Mario in the long screen journey which brought the extremist Benigni of *Berlinguer ti voglio bene* closer to the Chaplin-like hero of *Life Is Beautiful*. It was Nicoletta who made him less and less a Groucho Marx and ever more Chaplin, in an inexorable march towards this melancholic pathos. Nicoletta was the North Star, Nicoletta was the fairy tale of love.

Though basically emotional, this love not only manifests itself as a sentiment, but also as a beating muscle that bursts forth from the chest, a physical need that makes Benigni's heroes hyperactive and urges them to break all the rules, to erupt into the great hall of the Grand Hotel on a white horse, tearing his beloved from the arms of his rival, more sensationally even than

Panther when Blake Edwards gave Nicoletta a cameo role at the end of the film, as inspector Clouseau's daughter, the hero's sister. Braschi was Benigni's indispensable good luck charm.

It was not only a matter of affection (though the poor Nicoletta Braschi had to face quite a lot of loathing and unpleasantness as a "recommended actress"); but this was also Benigni's way of confirming his tendency to create a fixed persona for himself, a screen character, just like Charlie Chaplin, surrounding himself with recurring faces for character roles (such as Monni and Bonacelli), but above all that of his own partner.

Nicoletta was in any case a true actress, with classical drama training at the Academy and stage experience. Before being

> *My only true concern in any instance is to find where simplicity lies, to avoid banality. This seems easy, but in fact it is very, very difficult, since banality and simplicity are very close to one another, though there may be an abyss between them.*

Dustin Hoffman in *The Graduate* (1967). A physical love, though not solely sexual, which all of Benigni's characters possess, even the spiteful little devil Giuditta. The kind of love for which sex is an erection of the heart and despite this, does not make any concessions to the commonplace in cinema.

Like Chaplin, though Roberto appears to be much more faithful when it comes to love in his marriages, Benigni could not but marry his Paulette Goddard. Or rather (seeing things from the other side), he could not but have gone before the camera with his beloved bride by his side. And so Nicoletta, whom he had wanted on the set of almost every one of his films, became Mrs Benigni in 1991. She took up the role with all the lightness it called for. It was indisputable that being Roberto's partner increased her stakes as an actress and helped her to acquire points which were redeemable elsewhere, landing roles of varying importance in films such as *Mystery Train* (1989), *Sostiene Pereira* [Support Pereira, 1995], *Pasolini un delitto italiano* [Pasolini, an Italian crime, 1995] and *Ovosodo* [Hard-boiled eggs, 1997], in which she gave quite admirable performances. Nicoletta Braschi nevertheless remains a poetic and candid figure in the not-very-immaculate panorama of first ladies in Italian cinema.

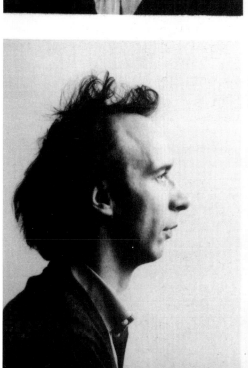
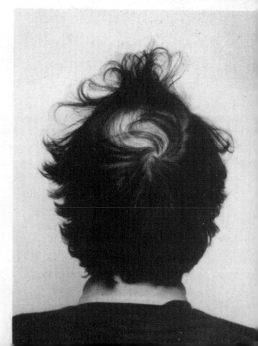

Is this the monster?

LET THE CHILDREN COME TO ME...

As is common knowledge, if you're a comic the best way to look at the world and its absurdities is through the innocent eyes of a child. Even Roberto Benigni adopted this ingenuous, amazed, curious gaze, though coloring it with his own spiteful side, like a street urchin, a little devil. He is Pinocchio, totally lacking in manners, who spreads his chocolate-covered hands all over the upholstery, who confuses and disrupts all established order.

We find him alongside children In many of his films: in *Chiedo asilo* he is a teacher, in *Tu mi turbi* an evangelical babysitter for Little Jesus. In *Non ci resta che piangere* he portrays an elementary school teacher, in *Johnny Stecchino* he is a bus driver for disabled children. He finally becomes a father in *Chiedo asilo*, but only when he confronts death. We would have to wait for *Life Is Beautiful* (1997) to see him fully take up this role. And he is a perfect father.

As early as *Chiedo asilo* Benigni had demonstrated how right the idea was of pedagogy based on games. With *Life Is Beautiful* the pedagogy of the game becomes the sole antidote to the most terrible drama in humanity: the mass extermination of a people. In this film Roberto Benigni portrays the role of a Jewish bookseller Guido Orefice, deported with his family to a concentration camp. There is also his son Joshua with him, a lively little child with a fondness for army tanks. His father

Guido manages to convince him that the horrors of the death camp are only a game. A very hard game in which adults and little ones compete in a match for points leading up to the final grand prize: a real tank, with tracks and cannons. Whoever complains loses points.

So little Joshua doesn't let even a tear slip, never asks for a snack, doesn't suffer, because he is protected by his father's imagination, who suddenly becomes a strolling player not by profession, but out of necessity.

Joshua's innocence is never soiled by horror or death. The little one manages to be saved, his father Guido does not. As in *Chiedo asilo*, Benigni dies at the end of the film, but in a solemn off-screen space, indicated only by a burst of machine-gun fire, without a cry or bloodshed.

Until just a few years before the film, no one would ever have dreamed they might see Benigni in a Nazi concentration camp. Legend has it that Roberto and his faithful screenwriter Cerami hit on the idea one ordinary evening in a little restaurant in the modest Roman neighborhood of Testaccio. A descent into hell such as this seemed unthinkable for a comic, yet Totò had also visited the inferno, and even the "magician" of entertainment Steven Spielberg (paradoxically one of the few people not to share in the chorus of praise for *Life Is Beautiful*) had made a film on it.

As everyone knows, nothing is more of a headache for directors than animals or children on the set. Apparently after the first weeks of filming *Life Is Beautiful*, about half-way

Left: *A moment of apprehension in the film* The Monster.

It is a film of great sensitivity, that expresses pain and love. The character of little Joshua is a triumph of optimism and life. I have never seen this expressed in a stronger way.
EHUD OLMERT, MAYOR OF JERUSALEM

through the shooting, little Joshua (Giorgio Cantarini, a young boy from the town of Montefiascone who has the same look as Comencini's little Pinocchio) was already fed up. He didn't want to have anything more to do with this business, something that had started out like fun but that was now just downright tiring. A fine problem for production. So Roberto decided to go for broke, he took him aside and said, "Look Giorgio, I know you can't take it anymore. After all, cinema isn't for everyone, it's a job only for those who are up to it… which means that tomorrow there'll be another little boy in your place. But since he doesn't look like you at all, he'll have to redo everything you've done up to now. No hard feelings though, I understand. It even happens to me sometimes, not to feel up to it and not to have what it takes to finish a job. Don't worry, go and play, it'll be for another time…" After a few hours little Giorgio came meekly back, "If you still want me, I can do it, I think I can go on with it now."

Benigni, as he had shown in *Chiedo asilo*, really did know children. That was one of the first obstacles he overcame on the path to the Oscar. But the biggest one was something else, of course – the scandal that *Life Is Beautiful* risked provoking.

It was true that there were subjects considered taboo for the entertainment world, yet one of the duties of a comic was precisely to break those taboos. "From today you are Jewish *honoris causa*," had declared the master of Yiddish comedy Moni Ovadia, expressing the feeling of gratitude with which the Jewish community had received *Life Is Beautiful*. The Israeli journalist Yossi Bar, Rome correspondent for the daily "Yediot Aharonot," gave profuse recognition declaring that Benigni was "capable of creating the incredible, a comic film on the Holocaust. Anyone else would have been accused of anti-Semitism." And the warm praise continued all along the route to the Jerusalem festival.

Though he was not Jewish, Roberto Benigni had learned many details of the camps from his father who during the last war had been interned by the Nazis in a work camp in Germany. "*Life Is Beautiful* does not claim any pretext to philological truth on the period or the concentration camps," explained Benigni, "it is a fable. The things that happen are based on truth, they come from the stories of two Auschwitz survivors who were on the set with me during the shooting, wonderful people who were able to speak serenely of what they had been through." Their names were Nedo Fiano and Shlomo Venezia, two Jews who miraculously survived the concentration camps. Their names appear in the credits at the end of the film.

Life Is Beautiful is clearly divided into two rather distinct parts: in the first half it presents "white telephone" Italy in rosy tones, with anti-Semitism growing little by little, though confined to the mood of a practical joke; in the second half, the action shifts to a concentration camp (reconstructed in an abandoned foundry near the city of Terni) and the tone of the story changes with a brusque turn to tragedy. When confronted with the dual soul of his film, Benigni gets out of it with another biblical quote: "If I may quote Ecclesiastes, there's a (first) time to laugh and a (second) time to cry."

In *Life Is Beautiful* Benigni benefits from the collaboration of a superb costume and set designer, Danilo Donati, Fellini's companion of fortune in visionary films such as *Satyricon* and *Casanova*. The hand of Donati, who is also a fine painter, is clearly recognizable in the chromatic character given to the two different parts of the film. When the story moves to the concentration camp, reality suddenly loses the colorful aspect it had shown up to then: it becomes despairing, almost black and white against a background from which the call to resistance

Benigni, Graham Stark and Liz Smith on the set of **Son of the Pink Panther.**

stands out even more starkly. For (as the title of the film declares), "life is beautiful," always, even paradoxically in the most tragic and darkest of all tragedies.

Conceptually the film was akin to the Dickensian Frank Capra of *It's a Wonderful Life* (1946) and Lubitsch's anti-Nazi comedy *To Be or Not to Be* (1942). In the beginning it was to be called *Buongiorno principessa*, a greeting the bookseller Guido Orefice, alias Roberto Benigni, repeats many times to his muse Nicoletta Braschi (who here, more than ever, embodies the universal idea of love). Thanks to the incessant promotional campaign conducted by Miramax to make the last sprint to the Oscars victorious, this became quite a catch-phrase in the States and particularly in the Italian-American neighborhoods of the big cities where Italian restaurants and pizzerias were even re-baptized "Buongiorno Principessa." In fact, "Life is beautiful" was a statement Trotsky entered at the end of his diary, after having related the unimaginable series of atrocities he had been subjected to in his existence. In short, in spite of the horrors, in spite of everything, life is beautiful. "It is a banal phrase if you say it lounging in an armchair," explains Vincenzo Cerami, "but applied to the most horrible of atrocities it becomes important."

"When the war ends," the screenwriter adds, "the little boy is in fact living the illusion that it had all only been a game. To spare him from the horror, the father preserves him from everything. And when peace returns, the little boy can continue to think that life is beautiful and more worth living than ever." *Life Is Beautiful* has the ambitious scope of a classic. And many observers have found in it the tone of Chaplin's *The Great Dictator*, another film in which a screen comic interprets the folly of Nazism in his own way. And Gian Luigi Rondi wrote that Benigni was the only comic to remind us of the great Chaplin. Roberto sent one of his compositions in verse to the legendary film critic who, in 1998 invited Benigni to receive the De Sica Award of the Five

Left: *Roberto before the great mystery of femininity (Nicoletta Braschi) in The Monster.*

> *When we went out location scouting I suddenly realized that I, as director, would always have to be present. This was something new to me, since I was coming from an actor's background where I never had to be there...*

Continents (we were at the peak of Roberto's season of prizes). A free translation of Roberto's poem might have gone something like this:

Wonderful Rondi / with the De Sica prize / You truly confound me / my friendly heart sighs. / But I can't come there / dear Giovanni Luigi, / From the 20th September / I'll be over in "Parigi."

The mixture of comedy and tragedy in *Life Is Beautiful* seems to be an old passion of Benigni's, who already in *Johnny Stecchino* and *The Monster* had wanted to treat two serious subjects in the form of comedies: in the former, the Mafia and in the latter, serial killers. "Fellini always used to tell me that only comics could take on tragedy without difficulty. Whether it was that they did it without rhetoric, or else because their rhetoric was so exaggerated that it didn't get in the way." Moreover, also Roberto Rossellini had gone this same route when he gave Aldo Fabrizi (at the time known only for his breezy characters) a tragic role in *Open City* (*Roma città aperta*, 1945).

A few rhetorical moments and slips into the pathetic might be reproached of *Life Is Beautiful*, something which often happened to the mature Chaplin, particularly in certain characters such as Calvero. And in this film once again the mise en scène sometimes appears slightly clumsy, particularly in the second half, where all the tension is concentrated on the people, and form tends to abdicate its role. But Benigni confirms his capacity to turn out films with a soul, not perfect but

It was as if my favorite team had won the inter-galaxy championship. Seeing him exultant on that stage had the same effect as when in '79, I saw him for the first time take up the mike at the Festival dell'Unità at Cascine, and watched him burst forth with all his vivacity. For us, as his young students, Benigni is like our Ronaldo, a spearhead. After this victory I hope there'll be more interest in other filmmakers too. It's like when back at school you had a really good friend and you said to him, "Go and see if there's a girl for me too."

LEONARDO PIERACCIONI, ACTOR

passionate, in spite of a simple "goody-goody" or even "Olive" vision as right-wing critics have reproached him, particularly Giuliano Ferrara's daily *Il Foglio*. The publication attacked the film violently accusing it of being subservient to left-wing power in Italy (perhaps the editor had never lived down being the butt of Roberto's jokes in his 1995-1996 tour and in the corresponding video edited by Cutry).

In September 1998, at the Venice Film Festival, the Rumanian film director Radu Mihaileanu pointed veiled accusations of plagiarism at Benigni. He claimed that one year before the making of *Life Is Beautiful*, he had had Roberto read his script *Un train de vie* (a group of Jews, to escape the concentration camps organize a false Nazi train for a pretended deportation of their fellowmen: Jews disguised as SS, a tragicomedy in Yiddish humor), and had wanted Benigni to act in it. Had Roberto Benigni read the script or not? Had the screenplay by

Opposite: *With Nicoletta Braschi and little Giorgio Cantarini in* Life Is Beautiful.

Radu Mihaleanu inspired him or not? Did it even at least get him to hit upon the idea?

In fact, to speak of plagiarism is quite an exaggeration, since *Un treno per la vita* [A train for life, 1998] and *Life Is Beautiful* are completely different in tone and story. Yet the coincidence of having two films in the same year treating the taboo of the Holocaust in the form of a comedy, does in fact seem strange. Roberto does not explicitly take a stance, though his collaborators have pointed out that scripts to be read arrive in mountains. In the end, the issue was not pursued since Mihaileanu did not wish pursue it.

All the Tumbles of a Tumbler

With the passing of the years Benigni has become more and more measured, increasingly less obscene in his speech, though he does not accept the all around "normalization" which his role as blockbuster and winner of several Oscars might impose. Roberto has not lost his liking for physical demonstrativeness. It might flare up at the first opportunity. His specialty still remains assault interviews, where the interviewer is practically "raped."

Benigni is like a child who has to touch everything, despite good sense and mother's constant scolding: "That's enough…!" All the presenters who have invited him as a guest on their shows have fallen victim to his ways, from Raffaella Carrà to Pippo Baudo, right up to the puritan American presenter David Lettermann, literally traumatized by the "long hands" with which Benigni stroked him during the program.

Having become famous for kissing and carrying Enrico Berlinguer, leader of the Italian Communist Party, off in his arms, and then for having kissed Walter Veltroni on the lips, Roberto came up with everything under the sun during the pre-Christmas promotional tour for the Italian release of *Life Is*

Opposite: *Roberto and Nicoletta on the set of* Life Is Beautiful.

When the director of the Italian Cultural Institute in Los Angeles asked me if I wanted to come and recite Dante I immediately said: "Mamma mia – of course! I'll recite Dante anywhere." For me, reciting Dante in Los Angeles was like Woody Allen reciting Walt Whitman in Viterbo. While I gazed out my hotel window at the wavering lights of Los Angeles, blurred by the smog, it occurred to me that I was exactly like Dante observing the flames of those souls in the Eighth Circle. Yes, Los Angeles was in fact Hell.

Beautiful (which was conducted by his faithful press agent Cristiana Caimmi as usual). He even took off his clothes on Enzo Biagi's live television program *Il fatto* [The Fact]. The scrupulous journalist gave an embarrassed smile.

When he later appeared on the channel TG1, at the height of prime time, Benigni simply could not stay put at his desk, and instead, jumped Giulio Borrelli in his starched shirt, like a furious Cioni Mario, desperately searching for any living being to take hold of, and then, kissing him, hopped on the table. It was quite obvious that in honor of the TV journalists in their jackets and ties, he would have liked to have proclaimed the *Hymn of a Loose Body*, those anarchic verses full of pure excremental obscenities. But he really just couldn't, at dinnertime, before ten million Italians sitting at table, in front of their soups. Calm down! That's quite enough. So Roberto threw himself into a furious improvisation of the main events in the news: cow breeders' protests against the imposed milk quotas. "I've spoken with

Prodi [then Prime Minister] who's my friend, about this and we've decided to settle the dispute with a trade-in policy for cows." You could just see Totò, Zavattini and Groucho Marx, his three patron saints, looking over his shoulder. Saints or maybe devils. Devils, yes. In Roberto's eyes there is still the flaming look of that little devil who stands up in defense of all our little devils, dulled by overdoses of newscasters, all so politically correct, who daily administer faded photocopies of the world to us for news.

Seven Nominations and Three Oscars

After Cannes '98, bestowing prizes on Benigni seemed to become an incurable disease. Juries on all five continents caught the virus and felt compelled to acclaim *Life Is Beautiful*. The film was very soon a veritable prize machine: Nastri d'Argento, David di Donatello, Prix César, European Film Academy Award, Globi d'Oro. Recognition at all the festivals, including the Festival of Jerusalem. Someone counted fifty-eight international awards, in addition to those received in Italy. And of course, the Oscar, the real one, bestowed three times upon Roberto by the people in "Olivood."

From Vergaio to the world. The globalization of the Benigni

I'm ashamed of these Oscars, other Italian actors deserved them, like Totò, Volonté, Peppino De Filippo, Mastroianni.

Giorgio Cantarini again in the film Life Is Beautiful.

*Roberto shows
two of his Oscars!*

The Oscar has brought bad luck to many actors.
So take your time and reflect on the future.
Leave the little films about provincial hoodlums
behind, and pay honor to this extraordinary victory.
FRANCO ZEFFIRELLI, DIRECTOR

phenomenon, which at first sight seemed quite impossible, happened much more effortlessly than expected.

Miramax, owned by the brothers Harvey and Bob Weinstein, the "adult" branch of Disney Productions and longa manus of the transatlantic Cecchi Gori, invested several millions for the launching of the film in grand style on the American market. Hundreds of copies: never had so many been made before in the United States for any other subtitled film. In the race to the Oscars the Weinstein brothers were betting on two films: *Life Is Beautiful* and *Shakespeare in Love* (1999). And they had also invested millions and millions in promotion. Steven Spielberg, who hadn't liked *Life Is Beautiful*, as a direct competitor of his own film, and perhaps fearing that it might cast a shadow on the myth of *Schindler's List* (1993), raised his voice to denounce the presumed immorality of so much hype. But it was a lost battle. For as long as people could remember, the Oscars had always meant out-and-out campaigning, quite similar to those of political elections: lunches, speeches, handshaking and lots and lots of TV.

Roberto took up an exhausting tour of the United States which kept him busy from summer 1998 until all of spring 1999, in countless cities. Official luncheons, endless interviews, talk shows, round tables, galas, parties, festivals, university classes, encounters with the Italian and Jewish communities. Roberto dining at Spago's with Liz Taylor and Rod Steiger. Roberto on TV dancing with Sarah Ferguson. Roberto cooking spaghetti alongside cordon bleu Sophia Loren. Roberto all over

Variety's big pages. His entourage shifted from one gala evening to another like a company on the road. He also performed some of his favorite numbers such as *Lectura Dantis* (a repeat of the reading he gave in Siena in 1990). This went to strengthen his "Italian" image – or Tuscan actually – as Dante Alighieri's fellow countryman and heir. The cream of American intelligentsia came to hear him on several occasions, packed into university classrooms and cultural institutes: academics, artists, writers. This Italian madcap reciting *The Divine Comedy* by heart was the most trendy thing ever.

Benigni, who had always adored Dante Alighieri (and who in tribute to the divine poet had baptized the hero of *Johnny Stecchino*, "Dante") recited the famous canto of Paolo and Francesca intensely and passionately, in a low voice, without exaggeration or mimics. Then, he went on to the canto of Ulysses, in a crescendo of emotion that left everyone breathless. Most of his public did not understand one word of Italian no less the fourteenth-century Italian of Dante Alighieri. But Roberto, before starting to recite, had reassured them in his simple but extremely effective English, "Don't worry. What's important is to feel the rhythm, even if you don't understand a thing – just like I did for many years." And then relieved laughter… the laughter from an America more and more in love with him.

In the New World Roberto also sold his image of a noble savage who, after great difficulties, had reaped the pleasures of culture. And this was the way he spoke of literature, in his own unique way, with the efficiency of an erudite peasant, cleverly mingling Hemingway and Boccaccio, Melville and Machiavelli, the Bible and *The Divine Comedy*. The Americans, with their pragmatism, appreciated this ability to synthesize, and most especially adored the concreteness of Benigni-thinking.

In the meanwhile, the powerful Jewish "lobby" of Hollywood, with Miramax's complicity and the Weinstein brothers' dollars, took up the cause of *Life Is Beautiful* and supported it in the annual rush to the Oscar. In the end, Miramax took home ten Oscars (seven for *Shakespeare in Love* and three for *Life Is Beautiful*), with Roberto Benigni managing to snatch one of the most prestigious of them all from Spielberg's Tom Hanks of *Save Soldier Ryan* (1998), the Oscar for Best Actor.

The box office also went along with Miramax, with *Life Is Beautiful* pulverizing all records in receipts of any Italian film in America, surpassing Salvatores, Tornatore, and even the monolithic Federico Fellini. In January the film had already exceeded 15 million dollars. By April, after its Oscar dividends, it was somewhere beyond the 40-million-dollar mark. On a worldwide scale, it had achieved receipts of over one hundred million dollars.

And today, as Claude Zidi's *Asterix and Obelix* is being launched on French screens (a colossal production, almost a French *Titanic*) in which Roberto appears in the role of the Roman Detritus, he must now face the question of how to manage the tremendous popularity brought to him by his Oscar-winning film. There are proposals galore, too many. Some producers are even waiting with blank checks. So many possibilities, so many risks, particularly the one of losing – in this torrential flood of dollars (according to the Wall Street Journal, after the Academy Awards Roberto's fee had risen to over five million dollars a film as actor, and three million dollars as director) – the roots of his own identity. And there are many who lie in wait for him.

FILMOGRAPHY

1977 *Berlinguer ti voglio bene* directed by G. Bertolucci (story, screenplay, acting)

1979 *Letti selvaggi* (*Tigers in Lipstick*), episode "Una mamma" directed by L. Zampa (as actor only)

1979 *Clair de femme* directed by C. Costa Gavras (as actor only)

1979 *I giorni cantati* directed by P. Pietrangeli (as actor only)

1979 *La luna* (*Luna*) directed by B. Bertolucci (as actor only)

1979 *Chiedo asilo* directed by M. Ferreri (collab. on screenplay and as actor)

1980 *Il Pap'occhio* directed by R. Arbore (as actor only)

1980 *Il resto del Pap'occhio* directed by R. Arbore (as actor only)

1981 *Il minestrone* directed by S. Citti (as actor only)

1983 *F.F.S.S. ovvero Che mi hai portato a fare sopra Posillipo se non mi vuoi più bene?* directed by R. Arbore (as actor only)

1983 *Tu mi turbi* directed by R. Benigni (dir., screenplay, actor)

1984 *Non ci resta che piangere* directed by M. Troisi and R. Benigni (co-dir., screenplay, actor)

1986 *Tuttobenigni* directed by G.Bertolucci (as actor only)

1986 *Down by Law* (*Daunbailò*) directed by J. Jarmusch (as actor only)

1986 *Coffee and Cigarettes* directed by J. Jarmusch – short subject (as actor only)

1988 *Il piccolo diavolo* (*The Little Devil*) directed by R. Benigni (dir., screenplay, actor)

1990 *La voce della luna* (*Voices of the Moon*) directed by F. Fellini (as actor only)

1991 *Johnny Stecchino* directed by R. Benigni (dir., screenplay, actor)

1992 *Night on Earth*, episode "Rome" directed by J. Jarmusch (as actor only)

1993 *Son of the Pink Panther* directed by B.Edwards (as actor only)

1994 *Il mostro* (*The Monster*) directed by R.Benigni (dir., screenplay, prod., actor)

1996 *Tuttobenigni 95-96* directed by Claudio Cutry (video)

1997 *La vita è bella* (*Life Is Beautiful*) directed by R.Benigni (dir., screenplay, actor)

1999 *Asterix and Obelix* directed by Claude Zidi (as actor only)

NOTES

Quotes from Robert Benigni have been taken from:
Stefania Parigi, "Benigni", Edizioni Scientifiche Italiane, Naples, 1988.

Roberto Benigni, Giuseppe Bertolucci, "Tuttobenigni", Theoria, Rome, 1992.

Massimo Martinelli, Carla Nassini, Fulvio Wetzl, "Benigni Roberto di Luigi fu Remigio", Leonardo Arte, Milan, 1997.

Roberto Benigni, "E l'alluce fu", edited by Marco Giusti, Einaudi, Turin, 1997.

Claudio Carabba, "Quella strana coppia", in Paese Sera, 13 February 1978.

Costanzo Costantini, "Toh, è morta l'ironia", in Il Messaggero, 18 March 1979.

Alberto Farassino, "E sul set una sorpresa: dovevo esserci sempre!", in La Repubblica, 2 February 1983.

Roberta Chiti, "Benigni, un comico sul serio", in L'Unità, 27 August 1989.

Carlo Boldrini, "Io, piccolo grande diavolo, vi dico che l'Italia", in Il Manifesto, 17 September 1989.

Gianni Manzella, "Pierino, il lupo e la gallina", in Il Manifesto, 13 November 1990.

Marco Molendini, "Alighieri, ti voglio bene", in Il Messaggero, 20 November 1990.

Roberta Chiti, "Commedia divina ed erotica", in L'Unità, 20 November 1990.

Eoberto Benigni, "Amo la gente di Cerami", in La Stampa, 12 May 1993.

Maria Pia Fusco, "Orco nazista, attento, Charlot è tornato", in La Repubblica, 12 December 1997.

Leonardo Cremonesi, "Formidabile lo sguardo di Benigni sull'Olocausto", in Corriere della Sera, 23 December 1997.

Cristiana Paternò, "Un poeta nel lager", in L'Unità, 12 December 1997.

Michele Serra, " Grazie Roberto", in La Repubblica, 19 December 1997.

Moni Ovadia, "Divertiti Roberto, da oggi sei ebreo honoris causa", in Corriere della Sera, 19 December 1997.

Daniela Sanzone, "Ti salverò da ogni malinconia", in Multisala, anno II, n.1, January 1998

Cabiria Pendleton, "Benigni legge Dante e trionfa a Los Angeles", La Gazzetta del Mezzogiorno.